LOST CIVILIZATIONS

A History of Vanished Empires and Forgotten Cultures

Bill Price

NEW BURLINGTON

Contents

Introduction

This book examines thirty-five historic examples of civilizations from around the world that have risen and fallen. Before reading on, let's take a moment to consider what the word "civilization" actually means. In dictionaries, it is often defined as "an advanced state with a developed society," which infers that civilization involves the presence of a complex social structure and a system of governance along the lines of that found in the nation-state today. It may also point to the presence of mass communication and a certain level of sophistication in the arts and sciences—even if, these days, we tend to forget that modern societies have a rather more down-to-earth foundation in agriculture.

In the past, archaeologists and historians have described humanity as following the path of progress: from simple to complex, from primitive to sophisticated, and from uncivilized to civilized. According to this view, human beings existed for thousands of years as simple nomadic hunter-gatherers who lived a hand-to-mouth lifestyle under the ever-present threat of violence and starvation. The invention of farming changed everything, allowing people to live in settled communities and to produce a surplus of food so that some people could specialize in trades other than farming. The ownership of property and the development of ruling elites followed, together with urban living and such innovations as the invention of writing. In more recent times, nation-states came together, run by governments and bureaucracies, so that we arrived at the civilized societies in which we live today.

As our knowledge of past societies has grown, it has become increasingly apparent that this model of a straightforward progression is not only too simple, but, in many respects, is fundamentally flawed. We have now begun to appreciate, for example, the complexity of hunter-gatherer societies, and how the adoption of agriculture was a slow transition involving numerous pragmatic decisions rather than a sudden revolution. And it surely only takes a brief glance at the world's modern history of devastating warfare and oppression to show that humans are barely any more civilized now than they have been in the past.

In light of such considerations, the concept of civilization has become much broader to accommodate people we may once have regarded as "primitive" or "uncivilized," and this is reflected in the civilizations examined in this book. In selecting the examples covered here, I have not applied any checklist of traits to distinguish what is and what is not a civilization—such as the presence of a particular type of governance, for example, or the use of the written word—so there are civilizations here from prehistory and from hunter-gatherer societies as well as from the ancient world and from more recent times. What these examples do have in common, however, is that they have all been "lost" at some point in time. Some disappeared from history only to be rediscovered at a later date, while others were once known before disappearing without trace.

Altogether, *Lost Civilizations* illustrates the fragile nature of the world in which we live. Today, we may like to think of our own civilization as being bulletproof, but the examples described in this book tend to suggest otherwise. Each one demonstrates that civilization is not necessarily permanent or stable; a wide range of circumstances can lead to its downfall, from war and conquest to climate change and the overexploitation of limited resources. All of these criteria have the potential to influence our lives in the future, especially if we fail to learn the lessons of history provided by these lost civilizations of the past.

Clovis Culture

Chapter One
PREHISTORIC CIVILIZATIONS

Proto-Indo-Europeans

La Tène Culture

Malta ●

● Göbekli Tepe

Indus Valley Civilization

The Natufians

This survey of lost civilizations opens with the Natufians, hunter-gatherers from the Eastern Mediterranean, who were among the first people to have lived in settled communities. From there, we travel around the world, visiting North America, Asia, and Europe as we explore those civilizations that disappeared before the invention of writing.

Did the Natufians Develop the First Civilization?

Where:	The Levant (the Eastern Mediterranean)
When:	12,500–9500 BCE
What:	A proto-civilization
Comment:	Good evidence that the Natufians were one of the first civilizations

ABOVE: The *Ain Sakhri Lovers*, a carved stone found in the Natufian site of Ain Sakhri caves, near the modern town of Bethlehem and currently at the British Museum, London.

Since it was first described in the late 1930s, the Natufian culture of the Levant has remained relatively obscure, at least beyond a small circle of academic archaeologists. Despite such anonymity, a case can be made for the Natufians developing into one of the first known civilizations in which people began to live in towns and cities. Beginning about 12,500 BCE, the distinctive culture flourished for something like three thousand years before it disappeared from the archaeological record, a loss that we are only now just beginning to understand.

A Sedentary Culture

The characteristic artifacts of the Natufian culture were first detailed in the 1930s by the British archaeologist Dorothy Garrod during excavations carried out on the remains of an ancient settlement at Shuqba cave in Wadi en-Natuf. It is from this settlement that the culture's name derives. The cave lies in the modern-day Palestinian territory of the West Bank, and subsequent excavations have found similar settlements and artifacts dispersed across much of the Levant, from western Syria and Lebanon, across Israel and the Palestinian territories and on into Jordan. Some of the most common finds include small stone tools, known as microliths, and seashells with bore holes drilled through them, which are thought to have been strung together and worn as ornaments. The style of these artifacts is different from those made by either the preceding or following cultures, enabling archaeologists to identify sites occupied during the Natufian period.

Natufian settlements were usually quite small, the largest having populations of around 150 to 200 people, and dwellings were simple, being made up of single rooms partially dug into the ground and surrounded by low stone walls. Wooden and brush structures are thought to have been constructed on top of

ABOVE: A typical example of a Natufian pestle and mortar, commonly found by the hearths in archaeological excavations of Natufian houses.

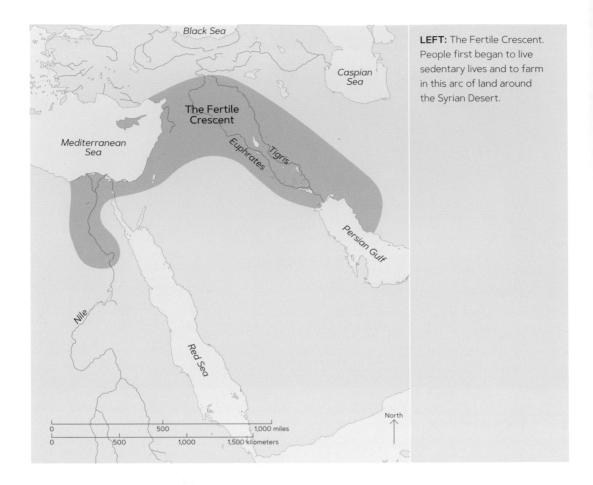

Black Sea

Caspian
Sea

LEFT: The Fertile Crescent.
People first began to live
sedentary lives and to farm
in this arc of land around
the Syrian Desert.

The Fertile
Crescent

Mediterranean
Sea

Euphrates

Tigris

Persian Gulf

Nile

Red Sea

North

| 0 | | 500 | | 1,000 miles |
| 0 | 500 | 1,000 | 1,500 kilometers | |

the stone walls to make roofs. What sets these dwellings apart from the sorts of
shelters built by previous cultures in the region is that the Natufians appear to
have lived in them either permanently or for the majority of the year. Before
this, dwellings were temporary structures, built in camps that were used by
groups of nomadic hunter-gatherers who moved regularly to take advantage of
different types of foods as they became seasonally available.

"Sedentism," as the practice of living permanently in one place is known, used
to be identified by archaeologists as being a particular feature of agricultural
society. Farmers, it was argued, had to stay in one place to manage their crops
and livestock, while hunter-gatherers needed to be nomadic to find food. The
evidence uncovered at Natufian settlements contradicted this idea because the
Natufians were hunter-gatherers who lived in settled communities. This has
lead to a fundamental shift in the way archaeologists view the transition from
hunter-gathering to farming.

The Beginnings of Civilization

It was once thought that the adoption of farming was the first step that happened in the progression of humanity from an uncivilized state in which life was, in the words of the political philosopher Thomas Hobbes, "nasty, brutish, and short," toward the sort of civilization that characterizes the modern world in which we live today. According to this view, the increased quantity of food available through agricultural production compared to hunting and gathering allowed people to specialize in trades and to live in towns and cities. It also led to population increases and to the development of stratified societies, in which ruling elites governed over such other classes as merchants and tradespeople. More complex societies could then develop, characterized by urban living and the emergence of the nation state. Archaeological investigations of the Natufian culture, and of those in other parts of the Fertile Crescent— the region of the Middle East in which farming was first practiced—have shown that the transition from hunting and gathering to farming and, by extension, the development of civilization, was by no means as straightforward as suggested by this simple progression model.

ABOVE: An illustration of an early farmer sowing seeds. The reasons why people changed from gathering wild grains to cultivation remain poorly understood.

The Natufians began living a largely sedentary lifestyle some three thousand years before the adoption of agriculture. This move to sedentism can, to some extent, be explained by the impact of climate change on the environment in which they lived. As the climate warmed toward the end of the last ice age, large areas of open woodland began to spread across the Levant. The grasses growing between the trees included wild strains of wheat and barley, together with many other varieties of food plants, and supported a variety of different species of grazing animals, including wild sheep and goats. This abundance provided the Natufians with food throughout the year, allowing them to stay in one place permanently rather than having to move as food sources became available in different areas.

Some archaeologists think that once the Natufians became sedentary, they may also have begun to manage the wild crops they were exploiting and, in doing so, began the process that would eventually lead to an agricultural way of life. If this was the case, the question remains as to why such a change was made. Finding food by hunting and gathering requires considerably less work than farming, at least where wild sources of food are readily available, so there must have been a good reason for the people who first adopted agriculture to take on this more arduous lifestyle.

One theory suggests that the transition to farming was a consequence of the climate suddenly becoming much colder around 10,800 BCE, during a period known as the Younger Dryas, which lasted for around one thousand years. This, according to the theory, reduced the availability of wild food resources in the Levant and in other regions of the Fertile Crescent, forcing people to adopt farming in an effort to ensure a more regular food supply. While this theory provides a reason for people taking on the extra burden of farming, the available archaeological evidence does not currently support it. In fact, the Natufians did not fully adopt farming as the climate got colder and, in some cases, actually returned to nomadic hunting and gathering. Agriculture does not appear to have replaced hunting and gathering until the climate began to warm up again toward the end of the Younger Dryas, by which time wild food sources were returning to the same sorts of levels found before the cold snap began.

In truth, we still don't know exactly why people first adopted agriculture, but one thing we can say about the Natufians is that once they had become sedentary, they began to use a similar set of tools as those adopted by later farmers. They used the same sorts of stone sickles to cut wild wheat and barley, and employed identical grinding stones to process grains into more digestible forms. Even if the Natufians did not farm themselves, the required technology was in place so that when the transition did occur, it may have been a smooth

THE BEER HYPOTHESIS

In 2013, evidence of beer brewing was found during the excavation of a Natufian settlement near the city of Haifa in Israel. It was dated to 11,000 BCE, making it the oldest known brewery ever found. It is thought the beer was brewed for ritual feasts, and the discovery of the brewery revived an old theory explaining why people first adopted farming. Providing beer for feasts, the theory suggests, may have been considered so important that people developed the techniques needed to grow wheat and barley themselves in order to ensure the availability of sufficient supplies rather than having to rely solely on what could be foraged from the wild.

and gradual one that did not cause a great deal of disruption to the way people lived their lives.

One Natufian settlement would later grow in size to become Jericho, sometimes described as the oldest city in the world. The oldest archaeological level found in the city dates to 9000 BCE and, by that time, the people who lived in the city were no longer hunter-gatherers, instead relying on farming for food. The artifacts from this period, known as the Pre-Pottery Neolithic A (PPNA), are very different than those found in Natufian settlements. One theory suggests that the Natufians were pushed out of their territory in the Levant by farming people who had migrated from other parts of the Fertile Crescent. But in recent years, advances in the collection and analysis of ancient DNA have allowed comparisons to be made between the Natufians and the farmers of the PPNA. The results have shown that the two groups were genetically very similar, indicating that, rather than disappearing, the Natufian culture adapted to living in farming communities and in larger settlements. In this respect, the Natufians can be considered a proto-civilization that was involved at the beginning of the transition and that eventually led to the fully fledged civilizations to come.

BELOW: Excavated houses dating to the PPNA at Tell es-Sultan, an archaeological site on the outskirts of the modern city of Jericho.

Why Did the Clovis Culture Disappear?

Where: North America

When: 11,000–10,600 BCE

What: One of the earliest American cultures

Comment: Reason for disappearance unknown but exhibited cultural adaptation

The Clovis culture is the name given to the people who produced a distinctive style of stone tool from around 11,000 to 10,600 BCE in North America. Examples of these so-called "Clovis points" have been found in many different sites across the continent, but were replaced in the archaeological record after 10,600 BCE by a variety of different styles of tools. This shift has led to speculation as to who the people of the Clovis culture were and whether other groups of people replaced them or their own culture changed over time.

ABOVE: The discovery of such distinctive Clovis points as the two shown here provides evidence enabling archaeologists to date sites to the Clovis period.

The First Americans

The Clovis points were first found in the 1930s at Blackwater Draw near the city of Clovis, New Mexico, together with a range of other tools made from stone and bone. The points were most likely mounted on shafts to make spears for hunting large animals, and could also have been used as knives. As more finds were recorded in New Mexico and subsequently in numerous other sites across North America, archaeologists began to speculate that the Clovis culture represented the earliest incursion of people into the North American continent.

The "Clovis first" theory, as it is sometimes known, argued that people originally entered North America by migrating from Siberia, traveling across what is now the open sea of the Bering Straits. They came via a land bridge, known as Beringia, which existed during the last ice age, when sea levels were considerably lower than they are today. At the time of this first migration, thought to have occurred around 15,000 BCE, ice sheets and glaciers prevented people from moving southward from Alaska. But by around 13,500 BCE, the climate had warmed sufficiently for the ice to begin retreating. An ice-free corridor opened up on the eastern side of the Rocky Mountains, allowing for the movement of people southward from Alaska into the rest of North America, apparently spreading out rapidly across the entire continent, which is why we now find Clovis points in such a wide variety of locations.

BELOW: Mountains overlooking the Bering Sea in Siberia. Beringia, the land bridge, was located here during the last ice age, when sea levels were lower.

Over the past few decades, a number of problems with the Clovis first theory have been identified, chief among them that archaeological sites thought to predate the earliest Clovis finds have come to light. If the dating of these sites is correct, and the Clovis culture was not the first to arrive in North America, the suggestion is that earlier inhabitants took up the technology the Clovis people brought with them soon after their arrival. This would account for the rapid spread of the Clovis culture across North America—in this scenario, occurring by a process of cultural diffusion rather than migration.

Doubts also exist concerning the possibility of Clovis people migrating through the ice-free corridor because very little archaeological evidence has been found in the region of the corridor to support the theory. Given the huge number of Clovis finds made at sites across the rest of North America, it would be reasonable to presume that similar sites should exist in the corridor, but so far none have been found. It is also thought by some archaeologists, that the

THE SOLUTREAN HYPOTHESIS

The Solutrean hypothesis suggests that the first people to migrate to the North American continent did not come from Siberia, but were actually European in origin. This is based on stylistic similarities between Clovis points and the stone tools associated with the Solutrean culture of Western Europe. According to the theory, at some point between 19,000 BCE and 15,000 BCE, European people traveled in small boats around the pack ice that then existed around the northern fringes of the Atlantic Ocean, until they reached North America. No archaeological evidence has been found to support this theory and the genetic analysis of Anzick-1 (see p.21) tends to refute it.

LEFT: This engraved stone from the Solutrean culture depicts a goat's head. It was found in a cave near Valencia on the east coast of Spain.

LEFT: The mammoth, one of the large mammals that became extinct in North America at about the same time that the Clovis culture disappeared.

corridor first opened at a later date than the first appearance of the Clovis points in North America, indicating that migration by this route would not have been possible.

An alternative route into North America has been proposed: Rather than going through the interior of the continent, it follows the coastline. Coastal areas may well have been ice free during periods of climatic warming and would have supported the dense kelp forests that can still be seen offshore in the region today. The kelp could have provided all sorts of foods for people as they migrated from Siberia and around the coast of Beringia to Alaska. So far, no archaeological sites have been found to support this theory either, but, as sea levels are now considerably higher, any evidence of people living on the coast at that time would be underwater today.

Little is known about the Clovis culture beyond what can be inferred from their stone tools. At one time they were considered to be nomadic hunters who followed herds of large mammals, such as the mammoths and mastodons that existed at the time. Today, archaeologists suggest that they would have exploited a much broader range of resources and are also likely to have gone fishing and foraging for edible plants. They also suggest that the evidence for this is lacking because they may not have used stone tools for such activities.

The Clovis culture only lasted for a relatively short period of time, perhaps five hundred years, before being replaced by a range of different cultures. One theory that attempts to explain this change suggests that Clovis hunters overexploited their environment by hunting large mammals to extinction. This theory, known as the Pleistocene overkill hypothesis, relies on the fact that many large mammals, including mammoths and mastodons, became extinct at roughly the same time and that this coincided with the period that the Clovis culture also came to an end. In causing the extinction of one of their main food sources, the theory suggests, they also brought about their own demise. This idea has attracted considerable criticism, not least because it is equally possible for the culture to have ended as a consequence of the extinctions as it is to have caused them, but also because the total population of North America at that time is very unlikely to have been high enough for hunting to have had such a dramatic impact. A more likely explanation is that the extinctions occurred as the climate grew warmer at the end of the last ice age, with forests replacing the tundra environment to which the mammals were adapted.

BELOW: Chiefs from the Blackfoot Confederacy of western Canada. DNA analysis has shown that First Nations people are descendants of the Clovis culture.

Anzick-1

In 2014, genetic analysis on the skeletal remains of a one-year-old boy found in Montana provided another source of information about the Clovis culture. The remains were originally found in 1968, scattered among various stone artifacts dating to the Clovis period, and were named Anzick-1 after the family who owned the land on which they were found. Anzick-1 was dated to around 10,600 BCE, right at the end of the Clovis period. After consulting with Native American people living in the area today, DNA samples were taken for genetic testing before the remains were reburied in the traditional manner.

Comparisons between the DNA obtained from Anzick-1 with samples taken from a variety of Native American populations in Canada and Central America have shown close matches, indicating that the people of the Clovis culture were most probably the direct ancestors of all modern Native Americans. Matches were also found with people living in Siberia today, confirming the theory that the first Americans came to the continent across Beringia, or around its coast, rather than by any other route.

So far, no comparisons have been made between Anzick-1 and modern Native Americans from the United States. This is because the motives of scientists are not trusted as a consequence of the past use of genetic data without the permission from the people concerned. Should relations between Native American groups and scientists improve in the future, it appears likely that DNA comparisons will confirm that all modern Native Americans are directly descended from the first people to live on the North American continent. This implies that the people of the Clovis culture were not replaced by other people and that, as they adapted to the various environments in which they lived across North America, the nature of their culture became different. The styles of stone tools found in the archaeology from later periods can therefore be seen as a reflection of these changes rather than a sign of the arrival of different cultures. As our knowledge of the Clovis culture increases, it is becoming increasingly clear that, though they were unknown to us before the first Clovis points were found, they are not really a lost civilization because their descendants are still living across the North American continent today.

What Was the Significance of Göbekli Tepe?

Where: Near Sanliurfa, southeast Turkey

When: 9500–8200 BCE

What: The dawn of civilization

Comment: Suggests a time of changing religious beliefs

ABOVE: One of the T-shaped pillars at Göbekli Tepe. Carvings of a vulture and an egg can be seen where the stone meets the top of the wall.

In June 2018, Göbekli Tepe was designated a UNESCO World Heritage Site in recognition of the remarkable archaeological discoveries made there over the course of the past few decades. The site stands on a hill overlooking a flat basin of land between the upper reaches of the Tigris and Euphrates rivers, not far from the city of Sanliurfa in southeastern Turkey, and contains the earliest known megalithic structures in the world. The site appears to have been used for religious rituals until it was deliberately covered over and abandoned some 1,300 years after its construction first began.

Monumental Architecture

The initial phase of building began at Göbekli Tepe around 9500 BCE, placing it right in the middle of the period of regional transition from hunting and gathering to farming. The types of stone tools and the animal bones found at the site show that these first builders were hunter-gatherers, while later work at the site was most likely carried out by some of the earliest farmers to have existed anywhere in the world. The fact that the site spans this transition from hunting and gathering—one of the most significant cultural shifts in the history of humanity—is what makes Göbekli Tepe such an important archaeological site. If we can understand what occurred here, then we will better understand a period sometimes described as the "dawn of civilization."

Excavations at the site began in 1996, under the direction of the German archaeologist Klaus Schmidt, who immediately found the first of several stone circles that have become characteristic of the site. In the decades that followed, three more of these stone circles were uncovered. Since only five percent of the site has been excavated so far, a great deal more work is yet to be done. In the meantime, geophysical surveys using ground-penetrating radar have been used to map the unexcavated areas and have shown that there could be as many as twenty circles clustered together across the site.

The stone circles excavated so far are each composed of ten or twelve large, T-shaped, limestone pillars that are surrounded by stone walls and have two further pillars facing each other at the center of the circle. The standing stones vary in height from 10–20ft (3–6m) and were quarried nearby before being transported the short distance to the site and set upright in slots cut into the underlying bedrock. This megalithic architecture is more than six thousand years older than Stonehenge, in England, which has led to Göbekli Tepe being described by UNESCO as, "one of the most exciting and significant prehistoric sites in the world."

The amount of work required to construct each circle—particularly given that the builders were using tools made from stone, wood, and bone —must have been enormous, demonstrating not only the great desire of the people living in the region at that time to build these monuments, but also their capacity to organize and manage a project that must have involved a large number of people working at the site over a considerable period of time. This has transformed our understanding of the hunter-gatherer society, once thought of as being composed of small bands of nomadic people. The people who began building Göbekli Tepe were, like the Natufians of the Levant, living in settled communities in large enough numbers that they could come together both to build the monuments in the first place and then to make use of them for what are thought to have been religious rituals.

No dwellings or any other evidence of sustained habitation have been found at Göbekli Tepe, leading archaeologists to conclude that it was principally a sacred site, used for ceremonies and rituals and, perhaps, for such social gatherings as communal feasts. The exact nature of the religious beliefs being observed remains unknown and can only be inferred from the archaeological remains. Numerous animals are carved into the stones, including lions, bulls, and vultures, and archaeologists propose similarities between the beliefs expressed at Göbekli Tepe and the shamanic practices of more recent hunter-

BELOW: An excavated stone circle, with ten T-shaped pillars surrounding two larger pillars, both of which have been broken at some point.

gatherer societies. Some of the stones are also inscribed with human hands and arms, which could suggest that these were intended to represent people, perhaps as part of the worship of venerated ancestors or gods in human form. In truth, with so much more of the site yet to be excavated, it is impossible to be certain about anything that may have taken place here.

Changing Beliefs

One possible interpretation of the archaeology at Göbekli Tepe is that it represents a shift from the belief system of a hunter-gatherer society to that of an agricultural one. The lives of hunter-gatherers remain rooted in their own environment, which provides them with everything they need to live. As such their religious beliefs reflect this in the veneration of animals and of the landscape within which the people live. Farmers, on the other hand, attempt to change and control their environment and tend to direct their religious beliefs toward those factors that affect them, but that are beyond their control, such as the Sun and the changing seasons. Such a belief system could be described as looking to the sky rather than the Earth so, where hunter-gatherers may have practiced the veneration of ancestors, in farming communities this becomes transformed into the worship of sky gods which, over the course of time, can itself change into the worship of a single god.

ABOVE: A pillar showing relief carvings of animals, in this case a bull, a fox, and a crane.

According to this idea, this shift in religious practice appears to be played out in the monumental architecture at Göbekli Tepe. For example, the stones bearing animal carvings suggest shamanic practices more commonly associated with hunter-gatherer traditions. Yet some of the stone circles appear to have been constructed in such a way as to be orientated toward the location of the rising Sun at the summer solstice, suggesting the influence of agricultural practices. Combined, the two indicate the start of a transformation from the beliefs of a hunter-gather society to a new faith based on the worship of the Sun.

People living around Göbekli Tepe gradually adopted agriculture, and their religious beliefs may have diverged further and further away from those of their hunter-gatherer ancestors. As this process continued, the religious importance of the site may well have declined until, around 8200 BCE, it was no longer relevant at all. At this point, people appear to have gone to considerable trouble to cover the site over, as if symbolically burying the old religion with a gesture of finality that allowed them to concentrate on the future. In the process, they also inadvertently preserved the site for archaeologists to rediscover and puzzle over today.

Theories about what took place at Göbekli Tepe remain highly speculative. Whatever the case, by the time the site was abandoned, farming had completely replaced hunting and gathering across the region. This transition is regarded as being vitally important in the development of the earliest civilizations, which first began to develop in the lower reaches of the Tigris and

BELOW: A view of the landscape at Göbekli Tepe, which is Turkish for "Potbelly Hill." A roof has been constructed over the excavation site to protect the archaeological remains from erosion.

NEVALI ÇORI

A similar archaeological site known as Nevalı Çori was discovered during preparatory work for the construction of the Atatürk Dam in Turkey. Standing on the Euphrates River to the northwest of Göbekli Tepe, the dam was completed in 1992. Salvage excavations carried out before the site was flooded uncovered a number of stone circles with T-shaped pillars. Unlike those at Göbekli Tepe, the circles were located immediately next to a village and the earliest phase of construction dated to a slightly later period. Nevertheless, it was a remarkable discovery, now unfortunately lost beneath the waters of the huge reservoir created by the dam.

RIGHT: A statue recovered from Nevalı Çori before the site was flooded, now on display in the archaeological museum in Şanlıurfa, Turkey.

Euphrates rivers in Mesopotamia. As such, Göbekli Tepe could be described as demonstrating the start of the process that led to the development of civilization and, as expressed by UNESCO, as "marking the very beginning of our modern lifeways and still prevailing world view." It also suggests that the dividing line between what we now describe as civilization and those cultures that preceded it is by no means as clearly defined as was once thought and that the hunter-gatherers who first began to construct the stone circles at Göbekli Tepe were, in effect, laying the foundations of the civilizations to come.

Who Were the Proto-Indo-Europeans?

Where:	Ukraine and Russia
When:	ca. 4000 BCE
What:	The first speakers of an Indo-European language
Comment:	Possible migrants to Europe and the Indian subcontinent

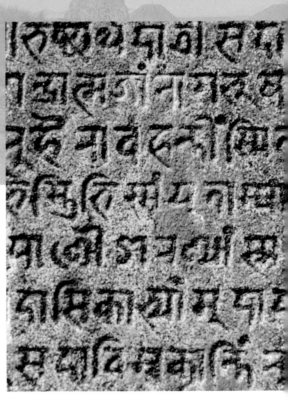

ABOVE: Sanskrit text inscribed in stone. The relationship between Sanskrit, Latin, and Greek was first proposed in the late 18th century.

Today, more than three billion people around the world speak a first language belonging to the Indo-European family, a group of related languages originally spoken from the Indian subcontinent to Western Europe and including, among many others, English, Spanish, and Hindustani. Since the relationship between these different languages was first noted, linguists have attempted to piece together their original root, which they call Proto-Indo-European. While this is a hypothetical construct, a real archaic language must have given rise to all the others. Since this original language must have existed, it follows that it was spoken by some people, who we could describe as being the Proto-Indo-Europeans.

The Kurgan Hypothesis

The relationship between a number of Indian and European languages has been recognized for centuries. It came to the wider attention of language scholars in the late 18th century through the work of Sir William Jones, a British judge and linguist who worked in India and was particularly interested in ancient Indian languages. In his work, Jones discussed the relationship between Latin, Greek, and Sanskrit—the ancient Indian language still used in Hindu religious services—and went on to propose further relationships between these and the Germanic and Celtic language families.

Ever since the relationship between Indian and European languages was established, linguists have attempted to reconstruct Proto-Indo-European, principally by comparing common words in different known languages— "water" and "house," for example—and extrapolating backwards to arrive at the original words. The resulting language may be entirely theoretical, but the nature of the words can be used to develop some idea of the life experiences of the people who would have used the original language, including aspects of their culture and religion. This is based on the type and frequency of words used to describe such practices as farming and religious observance. If, for example, the language contains words for "plough" and "horse-drawn cart," we can infer that the people who used the language were farmers who grew cereal crops and also made use of domesticated horses. When such linguistic research is put together with archaeological and genetic evidence, it becomes possible to develop an idea of where the language may have originated.

The most widely accepted of a number of competing theories on the origins of Proto-Indo-European is known as the Kurgan hypothesis, which was first proposed in 1956 by the Lithuanian-American archaeologist Marija Gimbutas. Based on the available evidence, she suggested that the language was spoken by people living in the region of the Pontic steppe, the huge area of open grassland to the north of the Black Sea and Caspian Sea, in modern-day Ukraine and Russia.

The reconstructed language pointed toward a culture in which some metals were in use, although not iron, leading to the conclusion that it had origins in the Bronze Age. It also suggested the presence of domesticated horses, and carts with solid wooden wheels. This led Gimbutas to propose a date of around 4000 BCE. Further linguistic evidence indicated religious practices involving the burial of the dead in underground chambers that were covered over with mounds of earth and stones. The evidence corresponded with the

archaeological finds of Bronze Age cultures of the Pontic steppe, where people buried their dead in such underground chambers, now known in the region as *kurgans*. Gimbutas used this name for the hypothetical culture she envisaged as speaking Proto-Indo-European on the Pontic steppe and it has since been adopted to denote her overall theory.

ABOVE: Two standing stones mark the entrance to a kurgan on the steppes of the Russian federal republic of Khakassia in southern Siberia.

The Yamna Culture

Genetic analysis carried out across Western and Central Europe, published in 2015, provided support for the Kurgan hypothesis and went further by tentatively identifying the actual people who may have been the original speakers of Proto-Indo-European. According to the study, DNA markers found in people across Europe today indicate that a wave of migration out of the Pontic steppe began around 3500 BCE, with large numbers of people spreading out across Europe and mixing with the indigenous inhabitants. This date corresponds with the period in which the Yamna culture was living on the Pontic steppe, whose cultural practices—including burying their dead in kurgans—also corresponds with the reconstructed evidence provided by linguistic studies.

The Yamna were skilled metalworkers. Some archaeologists consider them to be the first people to have domesticated the horse, although this theory is by

LEFT: Two anthropomorphic stone grave markers from the Yamna culture, found on the Pontic steppe of southern Ukraine and dating to around 3500 BCE.

no means accepted by everybody. Whatever the case, the horse allowed the Yamna to be highly mobile and must have contributed to their long migrations, which, it is suggested, could also have been the means by which Proto-Indo-European entered Europe. Further genetic studies have also established a link between the Yamna culture and northern India, strengthening the case that the language originated with them. One thing to note is that, although a great deal of information can be gathered through DNA analysis of past societies, one thing DNA does not reveal is what language the people being studied would have spoken. Despite such reservations, as we learn more about the Yamna culture, the evidence pointing toward its people being the original speakers of Proto-Indo-European is certainly becoming more convincing. At present, this identification remains circumstantial because it is not possible to say for certain what language they spoke, but the indications are that the languages of about forty percent of the people living in the world today can be traced back to the Pontic steppe.

THE ANATOLIAN HYPOTHESIS

An alternative theory to the Kurgan hypothesis suggests that Proto-Indo-European actually originated in Anatolia and began to spread to Europe around 6000 BCE, during the migrations that first introduced farming to the region. Genetic analysis confirms this movement of people into Europe, but the date is much earlier than the linguistic evidence indicates for the spread of the language. However, the Yamna culture was originally formed by the mixing of people migrating from both the north and south, including Anatolia, so the possibility exists of an even earlier form of Proto-Indo-European coming from Anatolia to the Pontic steppe, where it then evolved and dispersed at a later date.

What Happened to the Temple Builders of Malta?

Where:	Malta, central Mediterranean
When:	3600–2500 BCE
What:	Megalithic temple builders
Comment:	Reason for their disappearance is unknown

ABOVE: Monumental stonework at Ġgantija, the temple complex on Gozo dating to 3600 BCE, thought to be the oldest freestanding building in the world.

During the late Neolithic period, people on the Mediterranean islands of Malta and Gozo began to build large stone structures that we now describe as temples because they appear to have been used as places of worship and to carry out burial ceremonies. The earliest of these temples, Ġgantija on Gozo, dates to around 3600 BCE, and the building of similar temples continued for more than one thousand years. Then, around 2500 BCE, all of the temples were abandoned and the temple builders disappeared. Exactly what happened on the islands at this time has yet to be established.

The Temples of Malta

Altogether, around thirty archaeological sites on Malta and Gozo have been identified as megalithic temples. Some, like Ġgantija and the later sites of Ħaġar Qim and Tarxien, were excavated in the 19th century by amateur archaeologists, and much of the stonework remains as it did when first uncovered. Other sites are less well preserved, with just a few of the megaliths still in place, while there are a number that have yet to be fully investigated.

The basic plan of the temples appears to have been established at the earliest sites and copied at the later ones, with only a few relatively minor modifications. Each temple has an outside courtyard and a doorway made from three large stones that opens onto a central passageway. A number of semicircular rooms, known as apses, radiate off the passageway to form a floorplan with a cloverleaf pattern and these apses often contain a solid stone altar. In some cases, the altars have been decorated with relief carvings of plants and animals, or with a more abstract pattern of spirals and dots. At the best-preserved sites, such as Tarxien, similar stone reliefs adorn the external walls, while the internal walls show signs of having originally been plastered and painted with red ocher. Holes toward the top of the external walls are thought to have contained wooden posts to support roofs that have long since decayed away.

Large quantities of animal bones, usually those of sheep and goats, have been found in the apses, and archaeologists have taken these as evidence of ritual sacrifice and feasting. Numerous small statues have also been found, many of them depicting obese women. At Tarxien, the lower half of what was originally

LEFT: The entrance to one of the three temples at Tarxien. The use of three stones to make a trilithon doorway is typical of Maltese temple structures.

a life-size statue has survived, though it is not clear if it is male or female. These "fat lady" images, as they are known, are sometimes taken as an indication of the worship of a mother earth goddess on Malta and Gozo, which would most likely have involved ritual practices concerning fertility and birth. An extension of this idea suggests that society as a whole was matriarchal in nature, meaning that women held positions of power among the ruling and religious elites, though this interpretation is by no means accepted by all archaeologists. In recent years, excavations carried out at a number of the temples have found numerous burial sites in which people were apparently interred during elaborate funeral rites, leading to an alternative explanation to the mother earth theory in which the focus of religion was on death and burial rather than fertility.

Decline and Fall

Analysis of the skeletal remains recovered from the burial sites associated with these temples has shown that the diet of the temple builders was largely composed of meat and cereals. Despite living on islands, the people did not eat very much fish, instead relying heavily on agricultural produce. Such a dependency may have made them vulnerable to food shortages and famine in the event of poor harvests, and this could account for the disappearance of the temple-building culture after 2500 BCE. When farmers first occupied the islands in around 5000 BCE, the climate of Malta and Gozo was much wetter than it is today and the islands were covered with forests. The trees were cleared for farming, exposing the soils to erosion and a consequent drop in agricultural production. Subsequently, this may have led to the use of more intensive farming methods in an effort to boost production, which then became unsustainable as the climate began to grow hotter and drier toward the end of the temple-building period.

Some archaeologists have suggested that problems with food shortages could have been compounded by an increasing preoccupation with religious practices in which declining resources were used to build more and more temples and to conduct ever more elaborate rituals involving the sacrifice of

BELOW: The remains of the "fat lady" statue at Tarxien. Numerous smaller "fat lady" figurines have been found at Tarxien and at other Maltese temples.

THE HYPOGEUM

The Hypogeum of Ħal Saflieni is a complex of underground burial chambers that dates to the same period as the temples on Malta and Gozo. It was discovered in 1902 in Paola, a town across the Grand Harbour from the Maltese capital Valletta, and is composed of three underground levels containing about thirty chambers, many of which were cut into solid rock. It is estimated to have contained the remains of about 7,000 people and was in use throughout the temple-building period. Remarkable as the site is, it sheds no more light on what became of the people who excavated it than do the temples.

LEFT: One of the thirty underground chambers of the Hypogeum of Ħal Saflieni. It was cut into the solid rock using tools made from stone and antler.

animals. Rather than concentrate on maintaining a productive farming system, people were attempting to appease their gods and, if this was the case, it could have led to food shortages and the eventual collapse of society.

While such a scenario remains a possibility, nothing has so far been discovered in the archaeological records that can tell us about the ways in which people actually lived, so it is not currently possible to unravel the mystery of what happened to them. No villages and very few dwellings have been found, perhaps because these were constructed of wood rather than stone and have not survived. In truth, we currently have no clear picture of what brought the temple-building culture of Malta and Gozo to an end. What we do know, however, is that it caused the collapse of a highly developed and accomplished culture that has left some of the most extraordinary buildings constructed in prehistory.

What Caused the Decline of the Indus Valley Civilization?

Where: Pakistan and northwest India

When: 3300–1300 BCE

What: An advanced Bronze Age civilization

Comment: Possibly climate change or economic collapse

ABOVE: The upper reaches of the Indus River emerge from the Himalayan Mountains in the Ladakh region of northwestern India.

The Bronze Age civilization that developed in the valley of the Indus River and along its tributaries in modern-day Pakistan and northwestern India was contemporary with, and in many respects equal to, the better-known civilizations of ancient Egypt and Mesopotamia. Persisting for around two thousand years, from 3300 to 1300 BCE, its population, at its height, is thought to have exceeded five million people, many of whom inhabited well-developed cities. After around 1900 BCE, the civilization went into a decline that saw the cities abandoned. Archaeologists debate the reasons to this day.

An Advanced Civilization

The existence of an advanced prehistoric civilization in the Indus Valley was entirely unknown until the mid-19th century. Building work near the village of Harappa in what was then the Punjab province of British India unearthed old, baked, mud bricks and workers stumbled on the remains of buildings buried beneath the ground. Archaeological excavations of the site did not begin until the 1920s, at which point it became clear that the ruins of an extensive and previously unknown city lay beneath the soil. It was named after the nearby village and, as more settlements were found in other parts of the Indus Valley, it became increasingly obvious that this was not an isolated lost city, but an entire lost civilization. Initially, it became known as the Harappan civilization after the first site. Now that the full extent of the civilization is known to stretch the full length of the Indus River, along many of its tributaries, and fan out across its delta on the Arabian Sea, it has become more usual to refer to it as the Indus Valley Civilization. So far, more than one thousand settlements have been found, ranging in size from small farming villages to large cities that include Harappa, Mohenjo-daro, and the recently discovered Rakhigarhi, each of which are estimated to have supported more than 25,000 inhabitants.

ABOVE: Excavated walls at Dholavira, an archaeological site in the Indian state of Gujarat, where a city of the Indus Valley Civilization was discovered.

Archaeologists divide the Indus Valley Civilization into three periods based on the levels of urbanization and technological sophistication observed in the layers of excavation. An early phase is said to have begun around 3300 BCE, during which time farming villages began to develop into towns. Around 2600 BCE, this early phase progressed to a mature phase during which the population increased and towns grew into large cities. This phase lasted some 700 years and represents the height of the civilization. After 1900 BCE, a late phase began, characterized by a gradual decline that saw people abandon the cities and return to a way of life not unlike the early phase, with many of them living in small farming villages.

ABOVE: This Indus Valley Civilization seal, found at Mohenjo-daro, shows a unicorn and bears the undeciphered Indus Valley script across the top.

A striking feature of the cities built during the mature phase is the high level of urban planning that must have been involved during their construction. Streets were arranged on a grid pattern, with specific trades and crafts concentrated into different quarters of each city. Each dwelling was connected to a waste-water drainage system, which provided more advanced sanitation than found in the contemporary civilizations of Egypt and Mesopotamia. The cities of the Indus Valley also did not include such monumental buildings as pyramids and temples, suggesting that the society there was more egalitarian, even if the high level of urban planning evident in these cities indicates the existence of some form of centralized governance to coordinate and oversee the building work.

Most of the large buildings that have been found in the Indus Valley cities appear to have been communal granaries and warehouses, while archaeologists think that an enormous building found in Mohenjo-daro served as a public bath. No monumental tombs in any way comparable to the pyramids of Egypt have been discovered either, and though some burials are somewhat more elaborate than others, it would appear that the ruling elites were not treated very much differently in death than anybody else, just as they were in life.

Overall, little is known about the Indus Valley Civilization. It could be that archaeologists are less interested because it lacks pyramids and other monumental buildings. Another reason is that the so-called Indus script, which is thought to have formed a writing system, remains undeciphered. Numerous examples of this script exist on the thousands of seals that were used to impress symbols into wet clay, but it has not been possible to work out what these symbols mean. Unless a major breakthrough is made at some point in the future, the people of the Indus Valley Civilization are likely to remain anonymous to us, making it impossible to determine very much about the structure of their society beyond what can be extrapolated from the archaeology. For example, we know little about the nature of Indus Vally government. Neither do we know the names of any ruling dynasties or individual kings and queens. In truth, we don't even know if such dynasties or monarchies existed in the first place.

What we can say about the people of the Indus Valley, from the artifacts they left behind, is that they were highly accomplished metalworkers, creating numerous objects in bronze, tin, copper, and gold. The occurrence of these metal objects in the archaeology of other civilizations, including in Mesopotamia, together with a variety of distinctive ceramics, demonstrates that the people of the Indus Valley were engaged in trade over long distances. The discovery of harbors with docking facilities for large, seagoing ships in towns on the coast of the Arabian Sea provides further evidence that trade may have formed a vital part of the economy. The presence of a standardized system of weights and measures across the whole civilization—spanning some 1,000 miles (1,600km)—also supports this. Such coordination could also imply that the civilization was organized into a single political entity that could implement and maintain the system. Equally, it

THE DANCING GIRL

One of the best-known artifacts from the Indus Valley is the so-called Dancing Girl, a small bronze statue of a young woman striking a pose that suggests she is dancing. It was found during excavations at Mohenjo-daro in the 1920s and is now on display at the National Museum of India, New Delhi. When the statue was found, the site of Mohenjo-daro belonged to British India. Since independence, in 1947, Mohenjo-daro now lies in the province of Sindh in Pakistan. Some Pakistani politicians have called for the statue to be "returned" to Pakistan. The dispute over an object made some 4,000 years before the modern states of India and Pakistan were formed currently shows no sign of being resolved.

LEFT: The natural pose of the Dancing Girl is unusual for Indus Valley Civilization statuettes. She has bangles on her arms and her hair is tied in a bun.

suggests that the civilization could have been made up of separate city-states that maintained close relations between one another. One example of such cooperation can be seen in the baked mud bricks used to construct houses and other buildings. During the mature phase of the civilization, these bricks were of a uniform shape and size across the entire civilization, demonstrating a high degree of contact across relatively long distances.

A Time of Change

Our inability to decipher the Indus script, and the fact that many known sites across the region have yet to be excavated, have led to difficulties in establishing the cause of this civilization's long period of decline. Numerous theories exist and, though we know enough to discount some of these, none of those that remain can be confirmed either.

One discounted theory was first proposed in the 1940s. It envisaged an invasion of the Indus Valley by so-called "Aryan"people coming from the north. The theory came about following the discovery of the remains of human skeletons at Mohenjo-daro dating to the time when the city was abandoned. According to the archaeologists involved, the remains showed signs that the individuals had died violently and that their bodies had been left where they fell rather than buried. More recent research shows that this interpretation is just one of a number of possible scenarios, and that the most likely explanation for the presence of unburied bodies in the city, is that these people had died of disease once Mohenjo-daro had already been mostly abandoned. No evidence

LEFT: The mud-brick walls of Mohenjo-daro and the central Citadel, a public building containing baths, meeting halls, and residences.

of a hostile invasion of the Indus Valley has come to light, and while people certainly moved into the region from the north—perhaps bringing an Indo-European language with them—this probably occurred as a gradual migration over a period of hundreds of years.

The population of the Indus Valley certainly appears to have fallen during this late period, but rather than being a consequence of violence, it appears more likely that adverse environmental conditions caused a significant number of people to migrate away from the region, heading southeast toward the fertile lands around the Ganges River and its tributaries. This movement may have been a response to climate change, in which the seasonal monsoon rains shifted eastward, causing a drought that may have lasted decades, or even centuries, and that would have severely reduced agricultural production. Another possible explanation is the onset of an economic decline caused by the disruption of trading networks. The late phase in the Indus Valley Civilization coincides with a long period of political instability in Mesopotamia, which may have led to a major reduction in trade between the two regions. Such an interruption could have sparked an economic collapse and the kind of civil unrest that undermines the social cohesion required for a civilization to function properly.

Yet another theory suggests that there was not one specific reason for the decline, but a gradual accumulation of adverse conditions—perhaps including prolonged drought and economic instability—that made the continuation of urban living increasingly difficult. Some people may have migrated to the Ganges basin while others became farmers living in villages. If this was the case, then the people of the Indus Valley simply adapted to the changing circumstances they encountered. What we may now consider to be the collapse of the civilization may actually have been a perfectly rational response to a difficult situation in which the civilization carried on in a modified form.

At the present time, our knowledge of the Indus Valley Civilization is not sufficient to know exactly what happened to it. As research continues—in uncovering the archaeology of the region and in reconstructing the climate of the period—we gradually gain a better understanding of this great civilization of the ancient world. What is becoming increasingly clear is that the Indus Valley Civilization is not one that arose from nothing and then disappeared from history. Rather, it was part of the long and complicated story of the Indian subcontinent. Though its cities may have crumbled away, it has left a cultural inheritance that we are slowly beginning to appreciate more fully today.

What Happened to the La Tène Culture?

Where: From France to the Czech Republic

When: ca. 450–51 BCE

What: The Celtic culture of Europe

Comment: Declined following conquest by Rome and romanization of the culture

The La Tène culture of the Iron Age flourished in Western Europe for four hundred years, beginning around 450 BCE, and occupied territory across the middle of Europe from France to the Czech Republic. It is perhaps best known today by the surviving metal artifacts from the period, many of which exhibit a beautiful artistic style known as Early Celtic. The distinctive culture is sometimes said to have come to an end as a consequence of the territorial expansion of Rome, specifically with the conquest of Gaul in 51 BCE, but its influence would continue for centuries to come.

RIGHT: Typical La Tène style spearheads, dating to around 250 BCE.

Celts and Gauls

The La Tène culture left no written records, so what we know about it today comes from archaeological sites and artifacts, and from the accounts of contemporary Roman writers. We don't, for example, know what the La Tène people called themselves, or even if they referred to themselves as a collective entity. The culture was composed of numerous self-governing territories that may have shared common traits but that do not appear to have considered themselves part of an overall state. The La Tène name itself is modern, adopted by archaeologists after a site of that name situated at the northern end of Lake Neuchâtel in Switzerland, and where a large number of artifacts in the Early Celtic style were found in the middle of the 19th century. These finds led to the culture first being recognized as distinct from the earlier Hallstatt culture. Though the La Tène name is still in use, it transpires that the original site is actually dated toward the periphery of the culture rather than at its center.

The use of the word "Celtic" to describe both the La Tène people and their culture comes from Keltoi, the Greek word for the people of the region. The Romans later adopted the term as a collective name and, to add to the confusion, they also referred to the La Tène people as the Gauls or the Gallic tribes. In a further twist, "Celtic" came into usage in English during the 18th century in reference to the people of Ireland and the western fringes of Britain.

ABOVE: The Great Torque of Snetterton, found in Norfolk, England, and made around 100 BCE in the La Tène style of Celtic art.

The use of the same name came about after antiquarians noticed similarities in the style of Iron Age metalwork produced across the middle of the European continent with that made in Britain and Ireland. This led to speculation that Celtic people from the European continent had invaded the British Isles during this period, bringing their metalworking techniques with them. Perhaps they replaced the previous inhabitants, before later being pushed out of most of Britain by the invading Anglo-Saxons. There is no archaeological evidence to support either of these invasions, and while migrations certainly occurred, most archaeologists and historians now think that the similarities between the two cultures more likely came about as the result of the two regions being part of an extensive European trade network. Such contact may have involved the movement of a relatively small number of people, but led to both cultures influencing each other in such areas as the artistic styles used in metalworking.

Many of the metal artifacts from the period have been found in lakes and rivers, including at the La Tène site, and it is thought that these objects were deliberately thrown into the water during some form of religious ceremony. Beautifully made swords and shields have been recovered, which often display such intricate designs as to make them of little practical use. This suggests that these objects were either purposely made for ceremonial use or were symbols of power and prestige that were thrown into the water as offerings to the gods. Excavation of La Tène period burial mounds has also yielded artifacts, some of which have contained extensive grave goods. The preponderance of weapons and other fighting equipment in these burials gives an indication of the importance of military prowess within the La Tène culture, in which chieftains and elite warriors are thought to have maintained their status through military successes in battles and raids.

Distinguishing features of the La Tène culture include the two-wheeled chariots found in burial sites. The advanced design of these chariots, which were much more maneuverable than the four-wheeled carts used during the Hallstatt period, is thought to derive from the Etruscan culture of northern Italy, which was also part of the same trade network. The location of the La Tène culture at the heart of Europe placed it at the center of this network, where goods were exchanged from the Mediterranean region to Scandinavia and from Britain to what is now Turkey. The La Tène culture prospered as a result and, unlike their Hallstatt predecessors, who mostly lived in hill forts and farmsteads, the La Tène people began to live in large towns. Their increasing wealth can be seen in their jewelry, which has been found in burial mounds and in hordes, which were presumably buried as a means of keeping valuable objects safe. One type of artifact found in a number of these hordes is the torque, a solid gold neckband that is thought to have been worn by people of high status as a symbol of their rank and as a means of displaying wealth.

BELOW: A La Tène bronze torque from France, dating to 300 BCE and known as a "buffer type," due to the two flat terminals where the ends come together.

Conflict with Rome

Population growth appears to have prompted the La Tène people to take up urban living and it was also behind the migrations that began to occur around 400 BCE. It led to the development of Celtic regions in many other parts of Europe, from the Iberian Peninsula to Anatolia, and, as migrations occurred across the Alps into northern Italy, it also brought the culture into contact with the Roman Republic. This region of northern Italy was known to the Romans as Cisalpine Gaul and, despite periods of peaceful relations, raids by the Gallic tribes frequently led to armed conflict. The tribes sometimes formed alliances with each other to fight the Romans and on a number of occasions these alliances mounted full-scale invasions of Roman territory, several of which reached the city of Rome, leading the Roman Republic to consider them a serious threat.

VERCINGETORIX

Today, the most widely known person from the La Tène period is Vercingetorix, the chieftain of the Arverni tribe from what is now the Auvergne region of central France. In 52 BCE, he united the disparate tribes of Gaul in an alliance to fight against the invading Roman legions of Julius Caesar. After initial success, the Gallic tribes suffered a decisive defeat at the Battle of Alesia and Vercingetorix was taken prisoner. He was taken to Rome, where he was paraded during the celebrations of Caesar's conquest of Gaul and then executed. Gaul became three Roman provinces collectively known as Gallia and would remain under Roman rule for the following five centuries.

LEFT: The Vercingetorix Monument, erected in 1865 on the supposed site of the Battle of Alesia in the Burgundy region of eastern France.

LEFT: A reconstruction of a La Tène era farmstead at the archaeological site of Havránok in northern Slovakia.

By 225 BCE, Rome had become the most powerful force in Italy and was beginning to expand around the Mediterranean. It adopted a policy of northward expansion in an effort to put a stop to the threat posed by the Gallic tribes by driving them completely out of Cisalpine Gaul. In 192 BCE, after a series of wars, Rome succeeded in its ambitions by pushing the tribes back over the Alps and establishing Cisalpine Gaul as a Roman province. This can be regarded as the beginning of the end for the Gallic tribes. It was also the beginning of a long process of Roman colonization of northern Europe which, in 121 BCE, included the conquest of Transalpine Gaul, the region to the north of the Alps, and eventually to the invasion and conquest of the remaining regions of Gaul between 58 BCE and 50 BCE by Roman legions under the command of Julius Caesar.

After the conquest of Gaul, the territory occupied by the La Tène culture was in Roman hands. While this represented the end of the culture, its influence did not completely disappear. Instead, a hybrid Gallo-Roman culture emerged, in which elements of Roman social structures, lifeways, and cultural expression were taken up and absorbed alongside some of the older ways. The La Tène culture was gradually lost in this way and knowledge of it, beyond what the Romans wrote about it, remained hidden until it was rediscovered in the 19th century. The more we learn about it, the more it becomes apparent how complex and rich the culture was, and while we may now think of Western civilization as having its roots in ancient Greece and Rome, it is becoming increasingly clear that the La Tène culture also played an important role in shaping the world in which many of us live today.

The Olmecs

Moche Civilization

Chapter Two
ANCIENT CIVILIZATIONS

The Scythians

e Etruscans

Tuwana ●

The Minoans

Kingdom of Urartu

Petra, the
Nabatean
Kingdom

● Chengdu, Sanxingdui Civilization

Following prehistoric times, we now enter the ancient world to examine civilizations lost from around 3400 BCE to the early centuries of the first millennium CE. Coinciding with the invention of writing, this period marks the beginning of recorded history. Among the examples surveyed in this chapter are civilizations from ancient China, Turkey, and Peru.

Did a Volcano Destroy the Minoan Civilization?

Where: Crete, eastern Mediterranean Sea

When: ca. 3500–ca. 1450 BCE

What: An advanced Aegean civilization

Comment: Possibly suffered an economic collapse brought on by the volcanic eruption of Thera

ABOVE: The Cup-bearer Fresco from the palace complex at Knossos, reconstructed from fragments found during Sir Arthur Evans's excavations.

The advanced Bronze Age civilization on the Aegean island of Crete is known to us today as Minoan, and it is regarded as a forerunner of ancient Greece. Before archaeological excavations began on the island, at the beginning of the 20th century, the civilization was only known through references to it in Greek mythology. Since the extraordinary discoveries made during those excavations, our knowledge of the civilization, and its importance in the Aegean and Mediterranean region during the Bronze Age, has grown enormously. We still have a great deal more to learn, however, not least about the reasons for its sudden collapse.

A Discovery on Crete

In the Greek myth of Theseus and the minotaur, the Greek hero travels to Knossos in Crete with the intention of killing the minotaur, a creature with the head of a bull and the body of a man that lives at the center of a labyrinth in the palace of King Minos. With the help of Queen Ariadne, who gives him a ball of thread to unwind as he enters the labyrinth so that he can find his way out again, Theseus succeeds in killing the creature and escapes from Knossos, taking Ariadne with him.

ABOVE: The restored North Portico of the palace complex at Knossos. Altogether, the labyrinthine complex contained more than one thousand rooms.

When British archaeologist Sir Arthur Evans began to excavate a site on Crete, described by him as a palace, he named it Knossos and called the people who had built it Minoans after the mythical King Minos. No evidence has ever been found at the site to confirm any link with characters from Greek mythology beyond the fact that, as the full extent of the palace was uncovered, it was found to be composed of well over one thousand rooms, meaning it could be described as labyrinthine.

Today, archaeologists accept Evans's theory that the buildings at Knossos were associated with the Minoan ruling elite, and believe they had a much wider function in society than simply serving as the residence of the royal family.

The buildings are thought to have formed the civic, economic, and religious center of the surrounding city, also known as Knossos, and are estimated to have housed 100,000 inhabitants. Although Knossos was the largest Minoan city on Crete and is presumed to have been its capital, we don't known for certain how Minoan society was structured and several large palace complexes exist in other parts of the island, which may have been regional capitals or self-governing entities in their own right.

Our understanding of Minoan culture relies almost entirely on the interpretation of archaeological remains. Large numbers of clay tablets with writing inscribed on them show that, at the very least, a class of literate scribes existed, even if the vast majority of the population was unable to read and write. This writing system is known as Linear A and has not yet been deciphered. A second script, called Linear B, has also been found on clay tablets in the palace complex at Knossos.

ABOVE: This clay tablet from the palace complex at Knossos bears an inscription in the undeciphered Linear A script.

Deciphered in the 1950s, it proved to be an archaic form of the Greek language that only came into use after 1450 BCE. By that time, Crete had come under the rule of the Mycenaeans from the Greek mainland and, though the symbols used in Linear B are clearly related to those of Linear A, the latter appears to use a different and unknown language, making the process of deciphering it much more difficult.

Almost all of the deciphered Linear B tablets found at Knossos consist of what appears to be a system of accounting in which the contents of granaries and warehouses in the palace complex are recorded. Unlike in other parts of the ancient world, such as Egypt and Mesopotamia, no longer narrative texts have been found to provide us with such details as the nature of Minoan governance or the names of Minoan kings. The Linear A tablets look similar and are assumed to have served the same accounting purpose. Even if these are deciphered eventually, they may not give us a great deal more information about the Minoans than we already know.

The Mercantile State

The location of Crete at the southern extremity of the Aegean Sea played a crucial part in the developing wealth of the Minoan civilization. By around 2000 BCE, advances in design had increased the carrying capacity of ships and the distances over which trade could be conducted. Where Crete and the other islands in the Aegean had previously been restricted to trading among themselves and the Greek mainland, the larger ships allowed trade links to expand to include Anatolia, the Levant, Egypt, and other locations around the Mediterranean. Crete was perfectly placed to become a trading hub for this network, rather as Singapore and Hong Kong are in Southeast Asia today, and the Minoans exploited this opportunity to become very wealthy.

The palace complex at Knossos—and those in the other regions of Crete, at Phaistos, Malia, and Zakros—developed to the full extent now seen in archaeological excavations by around 1900 BCE. They were rapidly rebuilt following a major earthquake in around 1700 BCE, demonstrating that, at that time, such a natural catastrophe could be overcome. This was a period of economic boom, built on the trade of goods produced in Crete itself, such as wine, olive oil, ceramics, and a wide variety of other manufactured products, but also on the import and export of metals, timber, textiles, and other commodities shipped to Crete from all over the Mediterranean and sold on at a profit. To take just one example, the Minoans became the main suppliers of copper and tin, the principle constituents of bronze. They sold these to much of the rest of the Eastern Mediterranean region while also using the raw materials themselves, to make bronze items for their own use and for export.

BELOW: A Minoan ceramic jar decorated with a scene of marine life, a common theme found on pottery from this period.

Minoan trade outposts began to appear across the network, including on the Egyptian coast, where inscriptions have been found in which the Minoans are referred to as coming from the island of the Keftiu, though we don't know if the Minoans used this name for their island themselves. Settlements also grew up on mainland Greece and in the Levant. As well as traded goods, the Minoan style of arts and crafts spread out from Crete. The highly developed artistic skills of the Minoans can still be seen in the surviving frescoes at Knossos and Akrotiri, a Minoan town on the island of Thera, known today as Santorini. Akrotiri was buried under a thick layer of ash after an enormous volcanic eruption on the island, which preserved frescoes and numerous other artifacts later uncovered by archaeological excavations.

In around 1450 BCE, and after a long period of boom, the Minoan civilization came to an abrupt halt. Towns and villages were abandoned and many of the palace complexes were burned to the ground and not rebuilt. The cause of what appears to have been a sudden, catastrophic occurrence that overwhelmed and devastated the Minoan civilization to a point from which it could not recover is unknown and remains the subject of debate today.

The Collapse

One theory to explain the Minoan collapse is that the volcanic eruption on Thera could also have devastated Crete, which is some 60 miles (100km) south of the island. The eruption certainly destroyed the Minoan settlement on Thera itself and made the island uninhabitable, but the scale of its impact on Crete is less clear. Geological surveys have determined that a relatively small amount of volcanic ash from the eruption reached Crete, so it does not seem likely that this could have caused any great disturbance to Minoan farming. Such large eruptions can have longer term impacts because ash blown into the atmosphere can cause a rapid cooling of climate, which may then restrict agricultural production in the following years. Had this occurred after the Thera eruption, however, it would have affected a much wider area than Crete alone and there is no such evidence of this from other parts of the Mediterranean.

Another possibility is that the Thera eruption caused a tsunami that crashed into the northern coast of Crete, destroying its coastal towns and ports. As Minoan wealth relied on maritime trade, this would most likely have had a

BELOW: A cliff face on Santorini, originally formed by the Thera eruption, with the whitewashed houses of the modern town of Fira lining the cliff edge.

serious and potentially long-term economic impact, but it is by no means clear that it would have been enough to cause a total collapse. A further problem with the Thera eruption hypothesis lies in the dating. No consensus has yet been reached over the exact date of the eruption, but it most likely took place some time around 1550 BCE, roughly a century before the Minoan collapse. Furthermore, archaeological evidence of the Minoan civilization has also been found above the thin layer of ash deposited on Crete, giving the impression that any impact was not the direct cause of the collapse.

Although not the direct culprit, the eruption and possible tsunami must have weakened the Minoan economy and this could have been further compounded by both the loss of a significant trading post on Thera and widespread disruption to the trading networks across the entire region. At about the same time, Egypt was going through a long period of political upheaval, perhaps worsening the Minoan economic problems and contributing to what may have been a period of slow decline that would later leave the people vulnerable to attack and invasion from outside forces.

While we don't know if the Minoans were in decline after the Thera eruption, we do know that Mycenae was the emerging power in the region at this time. After the Minoan collapse, the archaeological artifacts found at Knossos become Mycenaean in character. This does not necessarily mean that Mycenae mounted a hostile invasion of Crete. They could simply have exploited the Minoan collapse to occupy the island by entirely peaceful means, taking over its central role in the highly profitable trading network. But the sudden nature of the end of the Minoan civilization and the fact that many buildings across Crete burned down at this time does suggest that some degree of violence was involved, even if the current state of our knowledge does not allow us to know if this was perpetrated by the Myceaneans or resulted from another, as yet undiscovered, cause.

THE MINOAN PEACE

During his excavations at Knossos, Sir Arthur Evans found little evidence of fortifications or military weapons, leading him to conclude that the Minoans were more interested in trade than engaging in armed conflict. He described the period of the Minoan economic dominance in the Aegean as the "Minoan Peace," and few signs of warfare from that period have since been found across the region to contradict this idea. So the Minoans may have been completely unprepared to resist any sort of hostile attack, perhaps presenting the Mycenaeans, who were certainly much more militaristic, with a relatively easy opportunity to take over the Minoan trade network by force.

What Caused the Sanxingdui Civilization to Move?

Where: Guanghan, Sichuan, China

When: ca. 1700–ca. 1100 BCE

What: A civilization in Sichuan province

Comment: An earthquake may have made the region uninhabitable

ABOVE: One of the bronze statues found in the sacrificial pits at Sanxingdui. It is thought to be the head of a bird of prey, possibly an osprey.

In 1986, a spectacular archaeological discovery in Guanghan, a city in the Sichuan province of southwestern China, led to suggestions that the history of early Chinese civilization may have to be rewritten. Thousands of artifacts in jade, ivory, and bronze—many of which had either been burned or broken up—were recovered from two pits. It appears they were thrown into the pits in a sacrificial ritual. The artifacts dated to the 12th century BCE, making them contemporary with the Shang dynasty of the Yellow River Valley, the earliest Chinese dynasty known through archaeological evidence.

The Sacrificial Pits

The most spectacular artifacts found in the so-called sacrificial pits include a collection of bronze sculptures and masks. Made using a method of metalcasting previously unknown in China, they exhibit a unique artistic style. The faces of the masks, for example, have highly exaggerated and angular features, with protruding, almond-shaped eyes that look more like the figurative paintings of Pablo Picasso than anything known from early Chinese civilization. The statues, made in a similar artistic style, include larger-than-life people as well as a wide variety of birds, animals, and trees. Altogether, the hoard represents one of the most exciting archaeological finds in modern Chinese history, perhaps second only to the discovery of the Terracotta Army, the sculpted soldiers numbering in the thousands and dating to around 210 BCE that were found buried in pits surrounding the unexcavated tomb of the first emperor of China.

At Guanghan, subsequent archaeological investigations have established that a city existed around the site of the two sacrificial pits, leading to the conclusion

BELOW: This bronze mask from the sacrificial pits is now on display at the Sanxingdui Museum in Guanghan, together with many other bronze artifacts.

that evidence of a previously unknown Chinese civilization had been discovered. This was named the Sanxingdui civilization, after the site, and tentatively identified as being the capital of the Shu Kingdom, a state located in Sichuan in ancient Chinese texts, but for which no evidence has been found to date. Any connection between the Sanxingdui site and the Shu Kingdom remains unconfirmed, but its discovery demonstrates that the development of Chinese civilization is more complicated than was previously thought. The standard version of Chinese history describes the Yellow River Valley as being the cradle of Chinese civilization, but historians now think that this should be broadened to acknowledge Sichuan, and perhaps other regions of China that have made significant contributions to the development of its civilization.

THE WUCHENG CULTURE

Bronze artifacts dating to 1200 BCE, the same period as those found at Sanxingdui, have also been found at archaeological sites in Jiangxi province. The sites are about 900 miles (1500km) to the east of Sanxingdui and are named after the town of Wucheng, site of the first finds. They include bronze masks bearing some resemblance to those at Sanxingdui, though many of the other bronze artifacts are clearly distinct. It is not known if there was any connection between the two, but it does demonstrate that Sanxingdui was not the only civilization in China to exist outside of the Yellow River Valley at that time.

A Move to Jinsha

In 2001, further significant archaeological finds were made at Jinsha, a site in Chengdu, the provincial capital of Sichuan, some 30 miles (50km) north of the Sanxingdui site. Artifacts showing a similar artistic style were found here, though in fewer numbers and dating to around 1100 BCE. It is thought that, sometime around 1150 BCE, the city of the Sanxingdui sacrificial pits was abandoned and its people moved to this new location at Jinsha. The reason why this happened is not known for certain and continues to provoke debate among Chinese archaeologists and historians.

Theories attempting to explain the move have included the possibility of an invasion by hostile forces or the occurrence of a major flood that made the city uninhabitable. If either of these theories is accurate, then signs would have been found in the archaeology of the Sanxingdui site and surrounding area, but nothing has so far come to light. Scientists at the Sichuan University in Chengdu developed an alternative hypothesis in the aftermath of the devastating earthquake that hit Sichuan province in 2008, causing huge loss of life and destroying many buildings. The scientists believe that an earthquake in the mountains to the west of Sanxingdui may have caused similar landslides to those that occurred in 2008, and that these may have obstructed the Min River, perhaps diverting its course and drastically reducing its flow at Sanxingdui. If this was the case, it would have affected the water supply to the city and the irrigation systems used to grow rice in the surrounding farmland, thereby making life in the city unsustainable and forcing its people to move elsewhere.

An earthquake and landslides in the upper valley of the Min River would not have left very much evidence in Sanxingdui itself, accounting for the apparent lack of disturbance seen at the site today. However, the scientists from Sichuan University have found indications that the Min River was much broader at Sanxingdui in the past than it is today, and they have uncovered evidence of historic landslides in its upper valley. The scientists also point to surviving texts from the Zhou dynasty, successors of the Shang dynasty in the Yellow River Valley, which refer to an earthquake occurring in 1099 BCE, although details of its location are lacking.

None of the evidence confirms the earthquake hypothesis and, so far at least, no written sources from the Sanxingdui civilization have been found. It is reasonable to assume that the civilization was literate because texts from the same period exist in other regions of the country. Should such discoveries be made in the future, it may be possible to understand why Sanxingdui was abandoned and to confirm the connection made between it and the Shu Kingdom, allowing us to understand a civilization that was completely lost to us before the discovery of the sacrificial pits.

LEFT: The Jinsha archaeological site in Chengdu, where artifacts similar to those found at Sanxingdui have been excavated.

What Caused the Disappearance of the Olmec Civilization?

Where:	Tabasco and Veracruz, Mexico
When:	ca. 1500–ca. 400 BCE
What:	The first Mesoamerican civilization
Comment:	Could have collapsed due to natural causes or food shortages

ABOVE: Stone statues found at the Olmec site of El Azuzul near San Lorenzo. A human figure is facing a jaguar, a characteristic feature of Olmec art.

The Olmecs were the earliest known of the great civilizations that developed across Mesoamerica, a region extending from modern-day central Mexico through Central America to Costa Rica, and predated better known civilizations such as the Aztecs and the Maya. The Olmecs began to emerge around 1500 BCE in the southern coastal region of the Gulf of Mexico, in what are today the Mexican states of Tabasco and Veracruz. The civilization lasted for more than one thousand years. By around 400 BCE, it was in terminal decline with cities becoming abandoned and the population dropping dramatically. The cause of this collapse has yet to be determined.

From San Lorenzo to La Venta

The existence of an advanced civilization in the hot and humid coastal regions of Tabasco and Veracruz was first recognized in the mid-19th century. Archaeological finds could not be dated at that time and the civilization became known as Olmec, after the Aztec word for the people who lived in the region at the time of the Spanish conquest, in the 16th century. The word means "rubber people" and the Aztecs used it because they obtained rubber from the people of the region, who made it from latex harvested from tropical trees. The name the Olmecs had for themselves remains unknown.

ABOVE: This colossal head from La Venta weighs 20 tons. It can now be seen at the La Venta Park Museum in the nearby city of Villahermosa.

The Olmec civilization appears to have emerged from earlier cultures in the region and first began to construct monumental buildings at San Lorenzo, which remained the major center of the civilization until around 900 BCE. The earliest of the so-called "colossal heads," a distinctive cultural feature, dates from this period. These were cut from single blocks of volcanic basalt rock, some of which came from the slopes of a volcano some 50 miles (80km) away. Most of the 17 known examples are roughly 10ft (3m) tall and have somewhat exaggerated facial features. They also wear what look to be helmets, perhaps signifying that they represent warriors or participants in the ceremonial ball game played by the Olmecs that later spread to other

Mesoamerican civilizations. Each head also has different features, and it could be that they are lifelike representations of Olmec rulers, although this theory cannot be verified and nothing comparable has been found anywhere else across Mesoamerica to help shed light on their significance.

After 900 BCE, San Lorenzo began to decline and the previously small settlement of La Venta developed into the largest city of the Olmec period. The reason for this shift is not known, but the apparent destruction of the buildings in San Lorenzo at that time could indicate that a war occurred between the two, from which La Venta emerged victorious. The most prominent feature at La Venta, despite 2,500 years of erosion, is the Great Pyramid that stood at the center of the city. It now resembles a grassed-over mound of earth, but is thought originally to have been a step pyramid similar to those built later by the Aztecs and Maya. This makes it one of the earliest buildings of this type constructed in Mesoamerica.

At its height, La Venta was the largest city in Mesoamerica and appears to have been the ceremonial center of the Olmec civilization. A large, open space described as a "plaza" lies to the south of the pyramid, and is thought to have provided an area for public gatherings, while a smaller plaza on the opposite side could have been a sacred space restricted to the ruling and religious elites. Little is known for certain about the nature of the religion practiced by the Olmecs. From the surviving sculptures and carvings, it would appear to have involved the worship of a number of gods based on natural phenomena, animals, and what are described as transformative figures— combinations of animals with either gods or humans. The two most prominent figures of worship appear to have been a rain god and a so-called were-jaguar, a divine figure with both

BELOW: This statue from La Venta is of an Olmec priest seated in a typical cross-legged pose. The damaged headdress was originally a jaguar's skull.

human and jaguar features. Evidence of ceremonial bloodletting also appears in stone carvings, together with what some archaeologists interpret as human sacrifice, a feature of several ceremonial practices seen in later Mesoamerican civilizations.

In recent years, a number of stone slabs inscribed with symbols have been found at Olmec sites, which some archaeologists propose represent a writing system. If this proves to be the case, then it will be the oldest writing found in Mesoamerica and could also possibly be the precursor of the writing system used by the Mayan civilization. However, no progress has yet been made in determining what these symbols mean and it remains unclear if they actually constitute writing. It has also been suggested that the Olmecs may have been the first to develop the so-called Long Count Calender used by the Maya, in which symbols represented numerals used to count the days. Again, the archaeological evidence is not yet clear enough to confirm this theory.

THE MIXE

The Mixe are one of many indigenous peoples living in Mexico today. They inhabit a remote place in the highlands of the state of Oaxaca, immediately to the west of where the Olmec civilization flourished more than two thousand years ago. The Mixe were never conquered by the Spanish. Their language and many of their cultural practices from the pre-Columbian period are still in use and it has been suggested that they could be the living ancestors of the Olmecs. The only way to confirm this would be through genetic analysis, but unfortunately no DNA samples from the Olmecs exist to enable comparisons to be made.

RIGHT: A Mixe woman and child, possibly living ancestors of the ancient Olmecs.

A Sudden Collapse

One reason for our knowledge of the Olmecs being more scant than that of later Mesoamerican civilizations is due to the fact that, unlike the Aztecs and Maya, the Olmecs did not persist into the modern period. Their civilization has also been less investigated by archaeologists, not least because, given the tropical climate of the region in which it flourished, only stone buildings and artifacts have survived while everything perishable, including human burial remains, has been lost. The gaps in our knowledge include the reasons for the collapse of the Olmec civilization despite other Mesoamerican civilizations continuing right up to the conquest of Mexico by the Spanish in the early 16th century.

BELOW: The Great Pyramid of La Venta, one of the earliest pyramids constructed in Mesoamerica. It has eroded to resemble a grassy mound.

Much Olmec territory appears to have become depopulated within a short space of time at some point around 400 BCE, when La Venta was abandoned and many of its buildings destroyed. This may have been the consequence of a civil war in which neither of the competing factions were strong enough to achieve an outright victory, so that the fighting continued until neither civilization could recover. Alternatively, the Olmecs may have suffered a natural catastrophe, such as a major earthquake or volcanic eruption, that disrupted their farming system to such an extent they were forced to migrate away from the region.

One other possibility is that, as the population of the Olmecs expanded after 900 BCE, the people began to overexploit their environment, causing a collapse in agricultural production that led to food shortages and famine. When land in tropical regions is cleared for farming, the soil is exposed to heavy rainfall, which leeches nutrients out of it and causes erosion. Where this happens, agricultural production can decline rapidly and the soil that has been washed away can lead to river systems silting up, causing the surrounding area to become marshy and infested with mosquitoes. If this was the case in the Olmec territory, then it is possible that their society reached a breaking point, forcing them to abandon their cities.

As the later Mesoamerican civilizations included several cultural and religious practices resembling those of the Olmecs, it is possible that the Olmec people migrated to other areas and assimilated with the people living there. Both the Maya on the Yucatán Peninsula to the south of the Olmec homelands and the Veracruz culture, which existed from around 100 to 1000 CE in the region immediately to the north of that of the Olmecs, were clearly influenced by them, but it is currently impossible to say whether this resulted from migration or cultural diffusion. Whatever the case, the Olmecs certainly began many of the cultural practices that spread to other civilizations and these persisted long after the Olmecs themselves had disappeared.

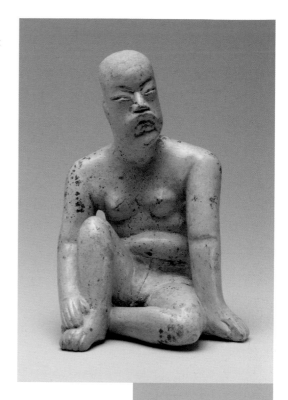

ABOVE: A typical example of an Olmec ceramic figurine. The elongated head and facial features indicate that it is a representation of a supernatural being.

Why Did the Kingdom of Urartu Suddenly Collapse?

Where:	Armenia, Turkey, and Iran
When:	ca. 900–ca. 585 BCE
What:	A kingdom lost for 2,500 years
Comment:	Reason for collapse unknown, but possibly the subject of an invasion

ABOVE: The site of the city of Tushpa, seen from the high ground of the Citadel of Van. Outlines of its buildings are clearly visible in the grassland.

Before archaeologists began to investigate eastern Anatolia in the early 19th century, Urartu, or the Kingdom of Van as it is sometimes known, was almost entirely lost to history. Neither the ancient Greek Herodotus nor any other classical historian mentions it, and the name only appears in a few contemporaneous inscriptions, providing little information about it. Urartu developed as a unified kingdom in around 900 BCE and flourished for the following three centuries before disappearing from history for 2,500 years. Even after its rediscovery, the turbulent modern history of the region restricted archaeological research so that our knowledge remains limited today.

Urartu Emerges

At its height in the ninth century BCE, the kingdom was centered on Lake Van, with its capital, Tushpa, on the eastern shore of the lake and Mount Ararat toward its northern boundary. The much larger and more powerful Assyrian Empire bordered Urartu to the south and the two states were frequently at war. Urartu, the name most commonly used for the kingdom today, comes from Assyrian inscriptions, while the people of the kingdom actually called it Bainili, possibly later corrupted to Van. The kingdom is also mentioned in the Bible, where it is named the Mountains of Ararat—most notably in the book of Genesis, where it features as the place where Noah's Ark came to rest after the flood waters began to recede.

Over the past few decades, archaeological research at a number of sites across the region has shown that the kingdom was a prosperous and influential one. It appears to have come together from a number of smaller kingdoms that began to merge after 1300 BCE, but it was not until 900 BCE that Urartu had grown strong enough to compete with the Assyrian Empire. Its wealth was generated through trade in such commodities as metalwork, wine, and horses, while its location allowed it to control important trade routes running between the Mediterranean, the Middle East, and Central Asia. At the same time, the kingdom developed into one of the region's strongest military powers, capable of defending itself against the threat posed by the Assyrian Empire as well as expanding its own territory. Ongoing archaeological excavations at the site of Tushpa and at the major regional city of Teishebaini near Yerevan, the capital of modern-day Armenia, have both found major fortifications situated on high ground. Such monumental buildings are a demonstration of the need for the Urartians to protect themselves against incursions into their territory, both from the Assyrians in the south and from other people from the north and east in what were most likely attempts to seize the considerable wealth of the kingdom.

In November 2017, a team of underwater archaeologists announced they had discovered a castle from the Urartu period under the waters of Lake Van. The

THE KELASHIN STELE

In 1827, the German Orientalist Friedrich Eduard Schulz found a stone slab in a mountain pass between Iran and Iraq, which bore inscriptions in both Assyrian and Urartian. The so-called Kelashin Stele, named after a village in the pass, proved vital in the decipherment of Urartian, a previously unknown language not related to the Indo-European languages spoken across the region. The text concerns the acquisition of an Assyrian city by the Urartian king Ishpuini, but the significance of the stele really lies in the role it played in allowing us to read Urartian rather than the message it carried.

observable fortifications of this castle are in a good state of preservation and are some 12ft (3.5m) high, though the extent to which these walls are buried in the sediment at the lake bottom has yet to be established. A large rise in water level during the last 2,500 years caused the lake to flood the castle and inundate a significant part of Tushpa. The city was, in fact, much larger than was previously thought and there could be an enormous wealth of Urartian archaeology yet to be discovered under the sediment at the bottom of the lake. An ever-increasing number of Urartian sites are being found as archaeologists investigate the wider region.

From Urartu to Armenia

The excavations at Teishebaini have established that, around 590 BCE, the city was destroyed by fire and abandoned. Archaeologists have unearthed the remains of granaries that appear to have been filled with grain shortly before the destruction began. They have also found scattered weapons and personal belongings of the type people would normally have taken with them, if they had left the city in an orderly fashion. The most obvious conclusion to these finds is that Teishebaini suffered a surprise attack that the people were not sufficiently prepared to repel, despite the city's extensive fortifications. While this interpretation is speculative, several candidates were capable of perpetrating the sort of destruction evident at the site and were known to have been present in Anatolia at the time.

The first of these, the Cimmerians, were a nomadic tribe of mounted warriors, known to have migrated northward through the Caucasus from their homelands on the Pontic steppe and then onto the Anatolia plateau. This would have led them into confrontation with the Urartu Kingdom because of its location between the Caucasus and Anatolia, but the migration is thought to have begun a century before the destruction of Teishebaini. While this does not exclude the possibility of a later attack by the Cimmerians, the more likely candidates are the Scythians, another steppe people who began to migrate southward through the Caucasus at a somewhat later date. Rather than move westward into Anatolia, however, they turned toward the southeast, where they are known to have come into hostile contact with the Assyrians.

No archaeological evidence currently conclusively links either the Cimmerians or the Scythians with the attack on Teishebaini, even if both groups were infamous at that time for mounting surprise attacks on wealthy cities. Neither does such an attack explain the collapse of Urartu as a whole, so a further possibility considers conflict with the Median Empire, the emerging power in

ABOVE: Ruined buildings are all that remain of Teishebaini, which was abandoned around 590 BCE after being destroyed by fire.

the region from what is now northern Iran. Media had been part of the Assyrian Empire, which collapsed in 612 BCE after several decades of civil war, and had established itself as an independent state. One possible scenario for the fall of Urartu is that, before coming into conflict with the Medians, it had been seriously weakened by the Cimmerians and Scythians and this was exacerbated by economic turmoil across the region, caused by the breakup of the Assyrian Empire. When not fighting against the Assyrians, Urartu was trading with its neighbor and the loss of such an important source of income must surely have had a severe impact. If this was the case, then the Median Empire may have taken the opportunity to invade Urartu while it was in this impoverished state and no longer in a position to defend itself.

Whatever the case, by 585 BCE Urartu was under the control of the Orontid dynasty, thought to have been indigenous Armenians who were allied with the Medians. The Orontids ruled the region as a client state of the Median Empire before being absorbed by the Persian Empire of Cyrus the Great, and then eventually emerging in 321 BCE as the independent Kingdom of Armenia. This encompassed the entire region previously occupied by Urartu and is now split between Armenia, Turkey, and Iran. Since the rediscovery of Urartu, it has held a special place in the national consciousness of Armenians. The sequence of events that led to its collapse and the establishment of Armenia may not yet be fully understood, but the ongoing archaeological excavations may eventually allow us to fill in the gaps.

Who Were the Enigmatic Scythians?

Where:	The Eurasian steppe
When:	ca. 900–ca. 200 BCE
What:	Nomadic pastoralists of the steppes
Comment:	Probably originated in southern Siberia and were then assimilated with other cultures

ABOVE: A Scythian gold pommel from the head of a sword handle, dating to the sixth century BCE and showing a coiled animal.

Today, the Scythians are best known for the beautiful items of gold jewelry and other ornaments that can now be seen in such museums as the State Hermitage Museum in St. Petersburg, Russia. Beyond the obvious fact that they were highly skilled in working with precious metals, little else is known about the culture of these ancient people. Debates that began with Herodotus and other classical historians continue today concerning who they were, where they came from, and where they went. Some extraordinary archaeological finds over the past few decades have led to a better understanding, but a great deal is still unknown and, in truth, the Scythians remain as enigmatic as ever.

The Eurasian Steppe

The Scythians appear to have emerged as a distinct culture around 900 BCE on the Eurasian steppe, the vast stretch of open grassland extending for thousands of miles from modern-day Eastern Europe to northern China and Mongolia. By around 200 BCE, they had disappeared, leaving very few traces behind them. In some respects, describing them as a "civilization" is stretching the definition of the word. They left no written records and built no cities, living instead as nomads who herded cattle and horses over vast stretches of the steppe grasslands, carrying their possessions with them in carts and living in camps they set up wherever they moved. They were also a formidable fighting force of mounted warriors, who showed great abilities as horsemen and archers and who could travel quickly over great distances to attack enemies or raid neighbors before melting away into the steppes again.

For the settled communities living in the vicinity of the steppes during this period, the Scythians represented a serious threat. Their incursions brought them into conflict with the great empires of that period, among them the Assyrians, the Persians, the ancient Greeks, and the ancient Romans. Herodotus, writing in the mid-fifth century BCE, devoted an entire book of his *Histories* to them. He thought they originally came from the Pontic steppe region to the north of the Black Sea, but also identified a number of other possibilities and several different groups, who he described collectively as being Scythian. The ancient Romans referred to all nomadic people from the steppe lands to the east of Western Europe as being Scythians, including those we now know as the Cimmerians and Sarmatians, leaving us with a confusing picture of exactly who was under discussion in classical literature.

Another issue that arises in trying to identify the Scythians is that they never constituted a single nation or formed any sort of recognizable state. They were a loose association of tribes with some shared ethnicity and cultural practices, who are thought to have spoken a number of similar languages, all of which had roots in the Iranian family of languages. One common cultural practice, shared with other nomadic people of the steppes, was to bury their leaders and elite warriors in mounds known as *kurgans*, a practice still seen in many regions of the Eurasian steppes today.

Scythian Gold

Nomadic people generally leave few signs behind them for archaeologists to study. Much of our knowledge about the Scythians has come from the grave goods found interred with them in their kurgans, which sometimes included large quantities of exquisitely crafted gold jewelry. In the early 18th century, the Russian tsar Peter the Great amassed a great collection of this jewelry, much of it recovered from kurgans in southern Siberia between the Ural and Altai mountain ranges. His collection forms the basis of the Scythian gold on display at the State Hermitage Museum. The jewelry provides a clear indication of the wealth of the Scythians, which they accumulated through raiding, the control

GELONUS

In the *Histories*, Herodotus describes a huge fortified settlement in Scythian territory to the north of the Black Sea, which was occupied by people of Greek origin he called the Gelonians. Some archaeologists think that the remains of massive earth ramparts near the village of Bilsk in northern Ukraine are the outer fortifications of this settlement, which they have called Gelonus and have described it as being the capital city of the western Scythians. Evidence of metalworking and other trades has been found within the site, so it may have been where some of the metal artifacts now associated with the Scythians were made, perhaps crafted by people of Greek origin rather than by the Scythians themselves.

BELOW: Earthworks near Bilsk, proposed as a possible location of Gelonus.

of trade routes across Central Asia and into Eastern Europe, and the trade in horses, for which they were particularly well known.

In the past, excavations of kurgans were mostly concerned with recovering Scythian gold. In more recent times, archaeologists investigating undisturbed burial sites have instead concentrated on what their overall contents reveal about Scythian culture. Some of the most significant finds have been made on a high plateau of grassland in the Pazyryk Valley of the Altai Mountains, which is near the intersection of the present Russian border with Kazakhstan, China, and Mongolia. Here, the graves beneath the burial mounds have been found in a remarkably good state of preservation because the underlying permafrost in this region has frozen any water seeping into the graves, effectively encasing their contents in blocks of ice and preventing the decay of perishable items. Textiles and artifacts made from leather and wood have been recovered, alongside gold jewelry and other metal items, such as weapons, helmets, and horse tackle. In one grave, food was found, including bread and cheese, while a woolen carpet had been preserved in another. The carpet was determined to have been made thousands of miles away in Armenia and has been dated to around 400 BCE, making it the oldest known carpet of its type in the world.

ABOVE: An excavated kurgan on the grassland plateau of the Pazyryk Valley, Siberia. The frozen mummy of a Pazyryk shaman was found buried here.

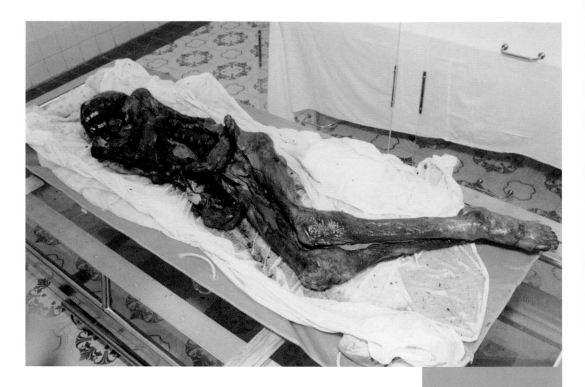

The Pazyryk burials also contained mummified bodies, some of which were quite well preserved. Best known, is the so-called Siberian Ice Maiden, the body of a young woman who was in her mid twenties when she died. She was found to have been suffering from breast cancer, though it is not known if this was the direct cause of her death, and was buried surrounded by six horses. Her skin, like most of the bodies recovered from the Pazyryk region, had been tattooed with intricate designs of animal motifs, a common feature in Scythian art, which may have related to her heritage and status. Despite newspaper headlines describing her as an "ice princess," the nature of her status is not known, even if her elaborate burial suggests that she was a member of the ruling elite.

ABOVE: The mummified remains of the Siberian Ice Maiden, found encased in a block of ice in a burial chamber beneath a Pazyryk kurgan.

Origins and Eventual Decline

In recent years, a combination of archaeological research and genetic analysis has been used to determine that the Scythian culture most likely originated in southern Siberia, not far from where the Pazyryk burials were found, before spreading out across the vast expanse of the Eurasia steppes. This does not necessarily mean that all of the people later referred to as being Scythian were ethnically Siberian because, as the original Siberian Scythians began to move out of their homelands, they mixed with other people across the steppe and with others from neighboring regions, so that hybrid cultures developed in which many of the original Scythian ways of life were retained.

By around 200 BCE, Scythian culture on the steppes appears to have come to an end. The reasons for this are currently unknown, but it could have been a consequence of the movement of people of different ethnicities into what had previously been Scythian territory. The Goths, thought to have been of northern European origin, began to move into the Eastern European steppes at about this time. In later centuries, Slavic people also began to migrate into Eastern Europe and what is today Ukraine and Russia. In the east, Turkic tribes began to expand westward into Central Asia, while the Scythians, who were in contact with the peoples of the regions to the south of the steppes, may gradually have become culturally assimilated until their way of life was no longer recognizably Scythian. Whatever was the case, the Scythians left a mark on the civilizations that were around them. While they may not have lived with many of the cultural trappings we now think of as denoting a civilization, they nevertheless produced some of the most beautiful works of art made during the period in which they lived.

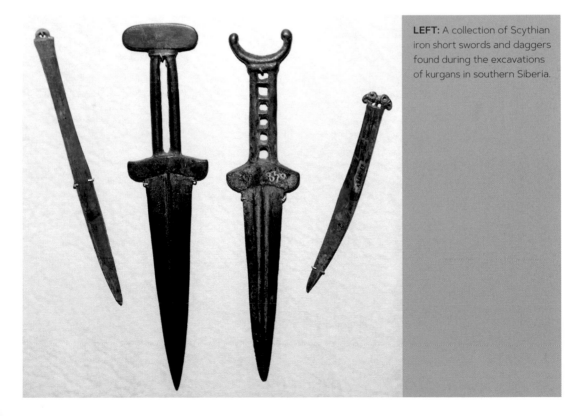

LEFT: A collection of Scythian iron short swords and daggers found during the excavations of kurgans in southern Siberia.

Did the Romans Destroy the Etruscan Civilization?

Where:	Western Italy
When:	ca. 700–ca. 100 BCE
What:	The civilization neighboring Rome
Comment:	Ultimately, the Etruscans were overwhelmed by the power of Rome

For the last two millennia, the noisier and rather more illustrious ancient Romans have overshadowed their neighbors, the Etruscans. Occupying a region of western Italy immediately to the north of Rome, in what are today Tuscany and parts of Lazio and Umbria, the Etruscans left a wealth of archaeological sites and artifacts behind them. Despite this abundance, we know little about this somewhat mysterious civilization. It is almost as if our knowledge of its culture has, rather like the Etruscans themselves, been overwhelmed by the power of Rome.

RIGHT: A beautiful example of an Etruscan bronze statue depicting a young woman.

The Unknown Etruscans

One of the central mysteries surrounding the Etruscans is where they came from in the first place. Unlike all of their neighbors, they spoke a language that was not Indo-European in origin and not related to any other European languages, leading to speculation that the Etruscans had migrated to Italy from somewhere else. The ancient Greek historian Herodotus, writing in the mid-fifth century BCE, thought they were originally from Lydia, a region of western Anatolia that is now part of Turkey. Four centuries later, Dionysius of Halicarnassus disagreed with Herodotus, instead proposing the theory that the Etruscan civilization was an indigenous phenomenon. Since that time, the debate has continued and, despite a number of genetic studies, it has not yet been conclusively settled. The balance of opinion favors Dionysius, whose theory is supported by DNA evidence and archaeological findings indicating that the Etruscan civilization probably developed out of cultures that had previously occupied the same region.

Unlike the ancient Greeks and Romans, the Etruscans left no substantial volume of written records. Almost all the Etruscan writing we have today comes from their tombs and is usually described by archaeologists as funerary text—it provides us with the names of the dead and excerpts of religious texts, but very little else. A number of ancient Greek and Roman writers mention Etruscan literature, leading some modern historians to suggest that, since such texts apparently existed in the classical period, they must have been destroyed intentionally by the Romans, rather than lost.

LEFT: A characteristic Etruscan tomb in the Banditaccia Necropolis, a UNESCO World Heritage site in the town of Cerveteri to the north of Rome, Italy.

LEFT: An Etruscan *bucchero* ware bowl from the late sixth century BCE. It would originally have been highly polished for a lustrous black finish.

The Etruscan civilization began around two centuries before Rome started to develop into the major regional power. The surviving Etruscan art and architecture demonstrates the cultural influence it exerted on Rome in that early period. Roman territorial expansion in the fifth century BCE brought its people into hostile contact with the Etruscans, and, over the course of the following centuries, led to the entire region coming under Roman rule. According to the theory, on gaining control of Etruscan cities, the Romans destroyed all written archives as a means of asserting their dominance and to obliterate any evidence that Roman culture was not completely Roman in origin. This idea perhaps owes more to the modern history of colonialism, in which dominant nations have attempted to subjugate others by destroying their culture, than it does to any actual evidence, but it could account for the mysterious absence of those written records that might otherwise have allowed us to gain a better understanding of the Etruscans than is currently the case.

Etruscan Art

With such little information available from written sources, we have to rely on what the archaeology can tell us, together with what can be gathered from the ancient Greek and Roman written sources. By far the largest architectural remains are the many tombs that can be found in cemeteries on the outskirts of Etruscan towns and cities. Typically, these tombs were cut into the underlying rock and had stone and earth mounds built over the top of them. Generations of the same family were frequently buried in the same tomb, often with extensive grave goods and elaborately painted walls.

As well as the funerary text, the interior walls of the tombs were often decorated with frescoes. Some of the finest examples of these tombs can be found in the Monterozzi Necropolis, a UNESCO World Heritage Site near the Italian town of Tarquini, some 45 miles (75km) to the north of Rome. The necropolis was the burial ground for the Etruscan city of Tarchuna, known to the Romans as Tarquinii. Altogether it contained 6,000 graves, 200 of which have frescoes painted on the interior walls. These include the so-called Tomb of the Leopards and the Tomb of the Dancers, both of which exhibit some of the finest remaining examples of Etruscan art.

A particular style of black pottery known as *bucchero* ware is a characteristic feature of Etruscan ceramics and, as well as being recovered from tombs, has been found all over the territory occupied by the civilization and in many other places around the Mediterranean with which the Etruscans traded. The discovery of bucchero ware in archaeological sites has been used to establish the extent of the civilization in Italy and to determine that the Etruscans were involved in a close trading relationship with the Phoenicians, who were originally from the Levantine coast and, at that time, controlled the largest trading network in the Mediterranean region.

BELOW: The frescoes in the Tomb of the Leopards, showing confronted leopards over a scene of feasting, thought to be a funeral banquet.

Equally characteristic of Etruscan archaeology are the beautifully crafted examples of metalwork, particularly artifacts made from bronze. Etruria, as the Romans called the Etruscan region, contained large reserves of copper and tin, allowing the Etruscans to engage in the trade of two of the most sought after raw materials of the period, and in the manufacture of their own bronze goods. They were particularly noted for their bronze statues—many of which were later looted by the Romans and most likely melted down for reuse—and for smaller items such as ornate polished bronze mirrors and decorated cylindrical containers known as *cista*.

THE CHIMERA OF AREZZO

The Chimera of Arezzo is one of the finest surviving Etruscan bronze statues. It depicts the chimera, a mythical fire-breathing beast with a lion's head, a goat's body, and a serpent's tail, and is thought to have been part of a larger sculpture showing the fight between itself and the ancient Greek hero Bellerophon. The statue was found in the mid-16th century in the Tuscan city of Arezzo, known to the Etruscans as Aritim. It was initially held in the collection of Cosimo de' Medici, the Duke of Tuscany at that time, and can now be seen in the National Archaeological Museum in Florence, Italy.

BELOW: The animated pose of the Chimera demonstrates the remarkable skill of Etruscan metalworkers.

Decline and Fall

The Etruscans grew wealthy on the proceeds of their trade in metals and other commodities. Their territory expanded and they founded new cities, including—according to some accounts—Rome itself. Though this is by no means certain, by the late seventh century BCE the Etruscans appear to have taken over Rome and governed the city until being ousted by a Roman resurgence. Over the following few centuries, the Romans went on to invade and capture much Etruscan territory during a long series of wars with individual Etruscan cities.

Etruria was not a united entity at any time in its history. Its city-states sometimes came together for the common good, but most of the time they were more likely to fight against each other than to unite against Roman intrusions. According to the funerary texts, each city appears to have been ruled by a powerful family or clan, in much the same way that the city-states of medieval and Renaissance Italy were ruled some two thousand years later.

The lack of cooperation between Etruscan cities made the entire region vulnerable as the power of Rome increased and, though we only have the accounts of Roman writers who were more interested in glorifying Rome than in establishing the facts, by 280 BCE the last major Etruscan city of Vulci had fallen. A process of assimilation followed, resulting in the decline of the distinctive Etruscan culture. The Etruscan language may have remained in use for a few more centuries, but by around 100 BCE the civilization had effectively ceased to exist. Today, it would perhaps be more accurate to describe the Etruscans as enigmatic rather than lost, because we know enough about them to be aware of the level of cultural sophistication they achieved, but also to realize that much of that achievement is now lost to us.

BELOW: The ruins of the city of Vulci, with a section of Etruscan road in the foreground. Vulci was the last Etruscan city to fall to the ancient Romans.

What Brought the Tuwana Kingdom to an End?

Where:	Anatolia, Turkey
When:	Eighth century BCE
What:	A city-state between the Phrygian Kingdom and the Assyrian Empire
Comment:	Reason for demise unknown, but perhaps invaded by the Cimmerians

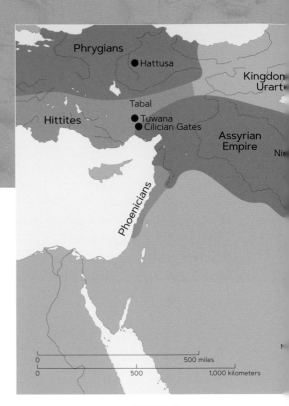

ABOVE: Tuwana was strategically located between the Phrygian Kingdom and the Assyrian Empire. It could also control access to the Cilician Gates, allowing it to levy taxes on travelers and merchants.

Before the discovery of archaeological remains at Kınık Höyük in 2012, the Tuwana Kingdom had been lost for more than 2,500 years. Our only knowledge of its existence came from a small number of monumental inscriptions found in southern Cappadocia, the region of central Anatolia where the discovery was made, and from records kept by the Assyrian Empire, which only provide us with the names of the kingdom's rulers. Now, as ongoing excavations begin to uncover the major settlement of the kingdom, the city of Tuwana, we have the potential to understand the role the kingdom played in the wider region.

The City-state

The city-state of Tuwana is thought to have arisen some time around 800 BCE, in a region that had once been part of the Hittite Empire. The collapse of the Hittites in 1178 BCE left a power vacuum across the region it formally controlled. The exact sequence of events leading to the rise of Tuwana is far from clear, but a city certainly stood on the site during the Hittite period. It is mentioned in the extensive archives discovered in the remains of Hattusa, the Hittite capital, in which it is named as Tuwanuwa. It continued to be occupied after the collapse of the empire, at which point the region became a patchwork of small, so-called Neo-Hittite states from which the independent city-state emerged.

ABOVE: The Cilician Gates, depicted here by the Victorian artist John Carne, were actually the ruins of a castle where taxes were collected from merchants using the mountain pass.

The city was located at the northern end of the Cilician Gates, a route through the Taurus Mountains known today as the Gülek Pass. The mountain range is a natural barrier dividing southern Turkey, separating the Anatolian Plateau from the plains of Cilicia on the Mediterranean coast, and the pass has been used for thousands of years to move between the two. It once provided a route for trade between Europe and the Middle East, making it a vital link on the Silk Road, the trading network via which goods from as far away as China were brought to Europe. It has also been of strategic importance—for example, Alexander the Great used it in 333 BCE, when he marched his army eastward to attack the Persian Empire. Controlling the entrance to the pass, as Tuwana did in the eighth century BCE, was a lucrative enterprise and led to the kingdom becoming very wealthy through trade and by levying taxes on merchants who had to travel through the kingdom to gain access to the Cilician Gates.

At the time, Tuwana was situated between the two major regional powers: the Phrygian Kingdom, which occupied most of central and western Anatolia, and the Assyrian Empire, based on the other side of the Cilician Gates at the city of Nineveh in what is now Iraq. The few written sources we have relating to Tuwana mostly concern the kingdom acting as a buffer state between its two larger and more powerful neighbors by sending ambassadors to one or the other to act as intermediaries. By the middle of the eighth century BCE, the city had become a tributary state of the Assyrian Empire of Tiglath-Pileser III, though it is not known if Tuwana was forced to pay tribute under threat of attack or if the much smaller kingdom did so as a means of maintaining friendly relations with Assyria without having to give up its independence.

Beyond the names of its kings, which include Warpalawas and Muwaharani, we know very little about the Tuwanan Kingdom from written sources. Around 700 BCE, the Cimmerians invaded Anatolia from the north, coming from the region of the Pontic steppe to the north of the Caspian Sea. They captured Gordium, the capital city of the Phrygian Kingdom and, Assyrian inscriptions tell us, they also attacked Tabal, the city-state immediately to the north of Tuwana, and Cilicia at the southern end of the Cilician Gates. No mention is made of Tuwana itself. While we can infer that it was also attacked by the invading Cimmerians, no details about what happened to the city are known. After the end of the eighth century BCE, the city effectively disappears from view for several centuries, before emerging again around 500 BCE, as a city within the Persian Empire. It would later change hands several times as the ancient Greeks and then the ancient Romans took control of the region. What happened in the two-hundred-year interval between the fall of the Tuwana Kingdom and the city being absorbed by the Persian Empire remains a mystery.

THE IVRIZ RELIEF

One of the few artifacts previously known from the Tuwana Kingdom, and the only known representation of a Tuwana king, is a rock relief in the foothills of the Taurus Mountains near the village of Ivriz. It marks the location of a spring and depicts King Warpalawas standing in front of the much larger figure of the weather god Tarhunzas. An accompanying inscription identifies the god as Tarhunzas of the Vineyard, and he is shown holding a bunch of grapes and a sheaf of wheat. The artistic style of the relief and the clothes worn by the figures are both Assyrian, suggesting that the relief was cut when Tuwana was an Assyrian tributary state.

Kınık Höyük

The excavations at Kınık Höyük have the potential to fill in some of the gaps in our knowledge of the Tuwana Kingdom and, more generally, what was happening across southern Anatolia in the long period between the fall of the Hittite Empire and the beginning of the classical period. The archaeologists involved in the excavations have described the site as being an acropolis, literally an "upper city," because it is raised above the surrounding land, where the remains of building work from the classical period, including a Roman aqueduct, can still be seen.

The site itself is composed of many different layers of archaeological remains, as new buildings were constructed over the top of older ones. This process continued until the site was finally abandoned at some point during the tenth century CE, leaving many levels from different periods, which makes the excavation of the site a complex one, not least because archaeologists are as interested in the more recent archaeology as they are in the levels dating to the Tuwana period.

Work is currently proceeding on these upper levels before it can progress to the levels of the earlier periods. So far, the remains of an ancient Greek temple have been found, together with pottery and figurines dating to around 400 BCE, placing them in the Persian period of occupation. Other ceramic fragments have been recovered that are in the style of the Tuwana period and the remains of the outer walls of the acropolis, which are thought to have stood about 20ft (6m) tall, are probably also from this period as well.

Geophysical surveys of the site, which provide an indication of what lies underground, have shown the presence of monumental building work within Kınık Höyük—possibly more temples from the Greek period or perhaps the remains of the royal palaces of Tuwana. Should this be the case, it would represent a major archaeological discovery with the potential to reveal the history of the kingdom. Other archaeological excavations in Anatolia and neighboring regions have found the archives of royal palaces and, should similar finds be made at Kınık Höyük, we may then be able to gain a better understanding of the relationship between Tuwana and both the Phrygian Kingdom and the Assyrian Empire.

Kınık Höyük occupies a site of around 50 acres (20 ha) and geophysical surveys indicate that the surrounding city was something like three times this size. Archaeological excavations in this "lower town" are only just beginning and could reveal the development of the city from the Hittite period to the classical one. The investigation of the site is an enormous undertaking and it may be decades before a complete picture of the occupation of the city becomes possible. In the meantime, we will have to make do with the knowledge that a lost civilization is finally beginning to emerge from the shadows, even if we will have to be patient before it is fully brought out into the light.

Why Did the Nabataean People Vanish?

Where:	Arabian peninsula, including modern-day Jordan
When:	Fourth century BCE–106 CE
What:	Vanished civilization
Comment:	Absorbed into the Roman Empire

ABOVE: The first glimpse a traveler gets of Petra when approaching it through the Siq, the narrow pass through the surrounding mountains.

The Nabataean Kingdom was established during the fourth century BCE, in the northwestern region of the Arabian peninsula, and expanded up toward the coast of the Mediterranean Sea. It flourished for approximately four hundred years, coming to an end in 106 CE, when it was absorbed into the Roman Empire. The remarkable monumental architecture that remains today in the ruins of Petra, the kingdom's capital, provides us with an indication of the wealth and sophistication of the Nabataeans. By the end of the fourth century CE the city had been all but abandoned.

Magnificent Ruins

Little is known for certain about the Nabataeans beyond what can be gathered through archaeological research because, unlike other civilizations in the region, they left few written records. It is thought that they were originally Arab nomads who settled into communities and used their knowledge of the surrounding area to control the water resources in what is one of the most arid regions of the world. Their territory encompassed the intersection of a number of important trading routes across the Arabian and Syrian deserts. Caravans of camels brought goods to Europe from China along the Silk Road and from the Arabian peninsula and Red Sea coast on the Incense Route, named after the lucrative trade in frankincense and myrrh that came from southern Arabia and the coastal region of East Africa.

The caravans traveled from oasis to oasis across the deserts, and the Nabataeans grew rich by exacting tolls on travelers and by engaging in trade themselves. In the first century BCE, they began a huge building project in Petra, during which most of the monumental buildings that can still be seen today were constructed. The best known of these buildings is the al-Khazneh, or the Treasury, which, despite its name, is actually the mausoleum of the Nabataean king Aretas IV. It was carved directly into the face of a sandstone cliff and positioned so that it was the first thing a traveler would see on approaching the city through its main entrance, the Siq, a narrow gorge that cuts through the hills surrounding Petra.

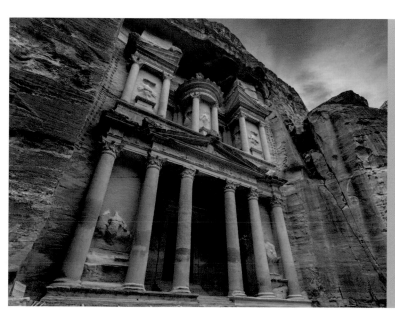

LEFT: The al-Khazneh, or the Treasury, is the mausoleum of King Aretas IV. The architecture of the facade was clearly influenced by that of ancient Greece and Rome.

Lost in the Desert

The architecture of Petra shows influences from ancient Greece, Rome, Egypt, Syria, and India, demonstrating that it was a cosmopolitan city, a melting pot of cultures brought together by the city's position at the center of extensive trading networks. At some point, the kingdom became a client state of ancient Rome and was then fully annexed into the empire in 106 CE by Emperor Trajan, becoming the Roman province of Arabia Petrea. The importance of Petra gradually began to diminish under Roman rule as the main trading routes to Europe moved away from the city so that, when a major earthquake struck in 363 CE, it was already in serious decline. Recent archaeological work suggests that the dams in the gorges surrounding the city were damaged by the

ADVANCED ENGINEERING

At its height in the first century CE, Petra is thought to have had a population approaching 30,000 people, a number made possible in such an arid place because the Nabataeans were highly accomplished hydraulic engineers. Water was piped to the city from springs in the hills, and dams were constructed in gorges both to store water for future use and to prevent flash flooding in the city after storms in the hills. Underground cisterns were also built to collect and store rainwater so that, altogether, Petra enjoyed such an abundance of water that the Nabataeans could afford to build large pools and fountains around their capital city. Making use of an otherwise scarce and precious resource in this way was probably not done solely for their own enjoyment; it was also a conspicuous display in which the Nabataeans demonstrated their wealth to the merchants and travelers who arrived in the city after crossing the desert.

LEFT: A section of the aqueduct bringing water to Petra from mountain springs. It allowed the Nabataeans to construct pools and fountains in the city.

LEFT: This lithograph of Ad Deir is by the Victorian artist David Roberts. Also known as the monastery, this is the largest of the rock-cut buildings in Petra.

earthquake and were not properly repaired afterward so that when heavy rain fell in the hills, the dams failed and a torrent of water cascaded through the city, causing even more extensive damage than the earthquake had done.

As the city fell into disrepair, it was gradually abandoned and, while the location of the ruins was known locally, Petra was forgotten by its former trading partners. In 1812, the Swiss Orientalist and explorer Johann Ludwig Burckhardt learned of the ruins of a city in the desert while traveling through the region and, on visiting the site, realized from the descriptions of Petra given by a number of Roman writers that he was standing in the remains of the Nabataean capital city. Burckhardt published accounts of the journeys he made through the Middle East, bringing Petra back to international attention after some 1,500 years of anonymity and leading to it becoming a popular destination for European travelers.

In more recent times, Petra has become Jordan's most visited tourist attraction and, in 1985, it was designated a UNESCO World Heritage Site. The romantic ideal of a lost city continues to exert a strong pull on our imaginations, even if the international attention now given to Petra has yet to translate into a wider knowledge of the people who built the city. The Nabataeans are still largely forgotten, remembered only for their extraordinary buildings and not for their kingdom or the central role they played in international trade. Petra may have been found, but the Nabataean civilization still remains lost in the desert.

What Caused the Moche Civilization to Disappear?

Where:	Coastal northern Peru
When:	ca. 100–ca. 700 CE
What:	An advanced South American civilization
Comment:	Destroyed by the impact of climate change followed by civil war

The Moche civilization existed for six hundred years, beginning around 100 CE in the coastal region of northern Peru and extending inland along river valleys. Its capital, also known as Moche, was at the mouth of the Moche River, near the modern-day city of Trujillo. At its height, the city had 25,000 inhabitants and included two enormous monumental buildings known as *huacas*, together with an extensive irrigation system to water the surrounding farmland. Around 550 CE the entire city of Moche lay abandoned. The civilization persisted for another 150 years before effectively ceasing to exist and it has only been in the last few decades that we have begun to understand why this happened.

ABOVE: This Moche pottery from a collection at the Metropolitan Museum of Art in New York is described as a "Raven Headed Figure Vessel."

The Huacas

The largest building in the city of Moche is known as the Huaca del Sol, the Temple of the Sun. It was constructed in several stages, beginning around 450 BCE, and is estimated originally to have contained 140 million adobe bricks. It has since suffered severe erosion and was also extensively damaged by Spanish conquistadors in the 16th century, who looted the many tombs it contained, so that, today, it could be taken for a naturally occurring rocky outcrop. The temple was built as a pyramid, with a ramp running up to a platform at the top, on which religious rituals were performed. A second, wider, platform at the pyramid's base accommodated the people who gathered to witness the rituals. As well as serving as a temple for religious ceremonies, the temple was the burial place of those who are thought to have been the ruling elites. It may also have contained residential spaces. A second huaca stands nearby—the somewhat smaller and less damaged Huaca de la Luna, the Temple of the Moon. Surviving murals on the interior walls suggest this huaca served as a burial site for the religious elites.

ABOVE: The eroded exterior of the Huaca del Sol in Moche. Originally a pyramid, this was the largest structure built in the pre-Columbian Americas.

The two structures were enclosed by a high wall and the remains of large houses have been found between them, suggesting this complex of buildings formed a compound for the Moche elites that was then surrounded by the residential areas of the city. Besides these monumental buildings, the Moche also constructed an extensive system of reservoirs, canals, and aqueducts to irrigate the farmland outside the city with water from the river. The entire coastal region occupied by the Moche is very arid and, to flourish here, they had to become masters of water engineering and irrigated agriculture.

Moche Treasures

In and around the two huacas, archaeologists have found numerous examples of the highly decorated ceramics and intricate metalwork characteristic of the Moche period. However, the looting of the tombs in the past has meant that what must have been extensive grave goods have long been lost. An idea of the riches these tombs contained can be gained from a number of intact tombs found in other Moche cities, including at the site of Sipan, which was found in 1987 and comprised three small and relatively untouched huacas. Among the finds was the mummified body of a man now known as the Lord of Sipan, who was buried with a wide array of metal objects, including a golden headdress, face mask, and extensive quantities of jewelry in gold, silver, and other metals.

The Lord of Sipan was buried with three women, who were dressed in ceremonial clothes and could have been his wives or concubines, together with two men thought to have been Moche warriors, and a child. All of these other people appear to have been ritually killed as part of the burial ritual, giving an indication of the high status of the Lord of Sipan and the practice of human sacrifice in Moche religious ceremonies. Further evidence of human sacrifice has been uncovered at the base of the Huaca de la Luna, where the skeletal remains of forty young men have been found, all of whom appeared to have suffered violent deaths.

BELOW: The mummy of the Lord of Sipan, with gold disks over his eyes. The mummy is now in the Royal Tombs of Sipan Museum in Lambayeque, Peru.

CHAN CHAN

The city of Moche is not the only remarkable archaeological site near Trujillo. The even larger city of Chan Chan, the capital of the Chimu civilization, can also be seen on its western edges. The Chimu occupied the same coastal region of northern Peru as the Moche had done, beginning around 900 CE and lasting until they were conquered by the Incas around 1470. The relationship between the Moche and Chimu is not clear, but the builders of Chan Chan certainly shared some of their predecessor's cultural practices, which can be seen today in the adobe brick architecture of their city and in the design of the artifacts they left behind.

LEFT: A street in Chan Chan. At its peak, the city contained 10,000 adobe brick buildings and was the largest pre-Columbian city in South America.

Murals found in a number of huacas, and the illustrations on some Moche ceramics, depict the enactments of battles that may have formed part of religious rituals, and in which losers were then sacrificed as offerings to the gods. Evidence also points toward the practices of ritual decapitation and the display of severed heads, bloodletting and the drinking of blood, and possibly even cannibalism. Such practices are considered extreme compared to those of other South American civilizations.

Another intact tomb was found in 2006, at an archaeological site known as El Brujo. It contained the mummified body of a young woman, the so-called Lady of Cao, who was elaborately dressed and accompanied by numerous grave goods, including gold jewelry and weapons. It is not known for certain if she was a member of the ruling elite or a priestess who conducted religious rituals, but, whatever the case, it indicates the likelihood that women held prominent positions in Moche society, which was not a common occurrence in other pre-Columbian civilizations.

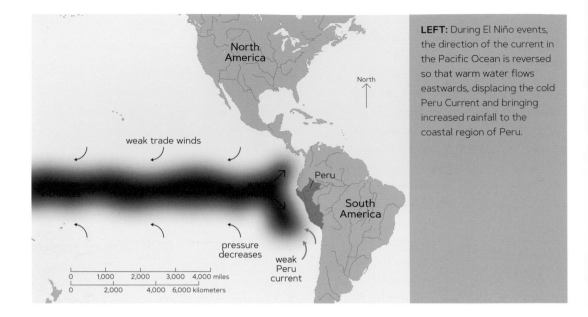

North
America

North
↑

weak trade winds

Peru

South
America

pressure
decreases

weak
Peru
current

| 0 | 1,000 | 2,000 | 3,000 | 4,000 miles |
| 0 | | 2,000 | 4,000 | 6,000 kilometers |

LEFT: During El Niño events, the direction of the current in the Pacific Ocean is reversed so that warm water flows eastwards, displacing the cold Peru Current and bringing increased rainfall to the coastal region of Peru.

The Impact of El Niño

The most likely cause of the abandonment of the city of Moche in approximately 550 CE, was a sudden change in climate brought on by a particularly severe El Niño event. El Niño involves a cyclical change in wind direction and currents in the Pacific Ocean during which warm water from the equatorial region begins to move southward down the western coast of the South American continent. This prevents the upwelling of cold water brought from the south by the Peru Current and, as cold water holds more oxygen than warm water, this results in El Niño reducing the overall productivity of the ocean. The impact on the coast of northern Peru is an increase in rainfall in what is normally a very dry region, and a reduction in the quantity of fish in the ocean.

Peruvian climate scientists have taken ice cores from glaciers in the Peruvian Andes from which they can reconstruct the past climate and this has confirmed that a particularly severe El Niño began in 536 CE and lasted for thirty years. The evidence in the city of Moche suggests that it experienced heavy rainfall and major flooding as a consequence, which could have overwhelmed the irrigation system on which its inhabitants relied for the production of food. The remains of the young men found at the base of the Huaca de la Luna were encased in mud, suggesting that they had been sacrificed during a period of heavy rainfall, perhaps in an attempt to appease the gods. The city appears to have been abandoned during this wet period and the climate data from the ice cores then indicates that the heavy rainfall was followed by thirty years of extreme drought. Sand from the dune systems along the coast was blown over the farmland and irrigation channels—apparently no longer maintained—and this prevented people from reoccupying the city.

This severe El Niño event may provide an explanation for the abandonment of Moche, but, as the civilization continued in other regional centers for another 150 years, there must have been another cause of its final disappearance. It is now thought that this was the result of a long period of civil war that began around 650 CE. The Moche were never united in a single state, rather being a loose confederation of cities and regions that shared similar cultural practices, and it is thought that the civil war was fought between these separate states as a result of political and social instability brought on by the long period of climate change that saw the regions compete with each other for dwindling resources. It is also possible that people began to loose faith in the religious and ruling elites who had failed to protect them from the excesses of the climate and, as new elites began to emerge in different cities, warfare erupted as they attempted to exert their dominance over others. Whatever the cause, by 700 CE the fighting resulted in many buildings being destroyed and only appears to have come to an end when the civilization had been devastated to a point from which it could not recover.

BELOW: A Chimu gold ear stud. The relationship between the Moche and Chimu remains unknown, but such artifacts show a clear cultural crossover.

Chapter Three
LOST EMPIRES

Empires rise when powerful states expand to take over the territory of others and, history suggests, persist for a certain period of time before falling apart. In this chapter, we describe great empires, such as those of the Akkadians and the Hittites, which not only rose high and fell hard, but that were then lost for many centuries before being rediscovered in modern times.

What Brought the Akkadian Empire Down?

Where:	Mesopotamia
When:	ca. 2350–ca. 2170 BCE
What:	Thought to be the first empire
Comment:	Possibly weakened by severe drought

ABOVE: The bronze head of an Akkadian ruler found in Nineveh, thought to represent either Sargon the Great or his grandson Naram-Sin.

The empire established throughout Mesopotamia by the Akkadian king Sargon the Great brought the disparate city-states of the entire region together for the first time. Because of this, it is sometimes described as being the first empire in history. Today, we know a great deal about this empire through written sources and archaeology, but there are still some holes in our knowledge. We don't know, for example, the location of Akkad, the empire's capital, or exactly what happened to bring the empire down less than two centuries after it began.

Sargon the Great

In the latter half of the 19th century, archaeologists made numerous discoveries in Mesopotamia that allowed them to piece together the ancient history of the region. Before that time, nothing at all was known about the Akkadian Empire and its first king, Sargon the Great, as he later became known. As archaeologists excavated the palaces of Mesopotamian kings, they discovered libraries containing archives of inscribed clay tablets and these provided a wealth of detail about the period. Tablets containing lists of kings are a common feature of ancient royal archives, perhaps compiled to demonstrate the heritage of the incumbent kings as a means of proving their legitimacy to rule, and Sargon was named in many such lists from the later empires of Babylon and Assyria.

To the Mesopotamian empires that succeeded Akkad, Sargon appears to have been a legendary figure, an example of how kings should conduct themselves and how empires should be run. Most of what we know about him today comes from texts written during these later periods, found in the archives of the Babylonian and Assyrian empires. But it is difficult to know the extent to which these texts were based on fact, or whether they were exaggerated to embellish the legend.

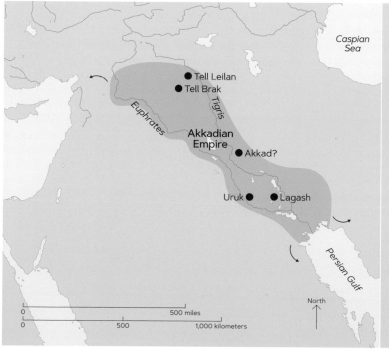

LEFT: The Akkadian Empire brought all of the Mesopotamian city-states together for the first time. Akkad is marked here as being on the River Tigris, but its location is not known for certain.

Clay tablets found in the library of Ashurbanipal, an Assyrian king from the mid-seventh century BCE, purport to be Sargon's autobiography in which he describes how he rose from humble beginnings to become king. He was, he tells us, the secret and illegitimate son of a priestess who could not keep her child and so was forced to cast him out onto the river in a reed basket. He was rescued by a servant in the king's household, who raised him as his own son. Sargon became one of the king's gardeners and gradually rose through the household on merit to become the king's cupbearer, a position we might now describe as the king's right-hand man. At some point, the king grew suspicious of Sargon for no apparent reason and attempted to have him killed. The king failed and instead Sargon deposed him and took the crown for himself. The story goes on to tell how, after taking the thrown, Sargon conquered other kingdoms until he had united all of Mesopotamia into one empire under his control. How much of this story is true is not known, but we can say that Sargon's empire certainly did exist, even if the way in which he acquired it is rather less certain. He established his capital city at Akkad and developed a system of governance and a bureaucracy of civil servants that became the model followed by later Mesopotamian empires.

ABOVE: Cuneiform letter from Canaan to Egypt.

The Curse of Akkad

Sargon is reputed to have ruled his empire for 56 years and was followed by two of his sons in succession. After his death, the empire went into decline until his grandson Naram-Sin ascended to the throne, beginning a series of military conquests to take back those parts of the empire that had been lost. One legend tells how Naram-Sin offended the Sumerian god Enlil; desecrating a temple after capturing the city of Nippur, he brought down the Curse of Akkad on the empire. According to the legend, the clouds did not rain and there were no crops in the fields and no fruit in the orchards so that the people began to die from hunger.

AKKAD

The sites of almost all major cities of ancient Mesopotamia are known and have been excavated by archaeologists. The exception is Akkad, which may have been founded by Sargon as the royal and administrative center of his empire. Opinions now differ as to its location. Some archaeologists propose that it stood on the Tigris River near the modern Iraqi capital of Baghdad, while others think it was on the banks of the Euphrates River. If Sargon built a library in his palace, should Akkad be found, its archive could still remain because the clay tablets used to write on at that time are incredibly durable.

Climate scientists who have studied the region note that a severe drought began in Mesopotamia around 2200 BCE and lasted for several hundred years. The data used in confirming this was gathered from sediment cores taken in the Gulf of Oman and has been corroborated by evidence collected at an archaeological site called Tell Leilan in northeastern Syria. It has been established that agricultural production collapsed at Tell Leilan around 2200 BCE, when increased aridity and a thick layer of sand blowing over the site forced most of the people living there to abandon it. Drought also appears to have had an impact in the wider region, including on the Indus Valley Civilization in what is now Pakistan, which began a decline in 1900 BCE from which it never fully recovered.

Naram-Sin's rule is thought to have lasted from 2254 to 2218 BCE, and by 2170 BCE the empire had been invaded by the Gutians—people from the Zagros Mountains to the east of Mesopotamia about whom very little is known. So, whether a curse was involved or not, a drought may have played a pivotal role in the fall of the Akkadian Empire, perhaps causing food shortages that weakened the Akkadians and left the empire vulnerable to people who would not have dared attack at its height under Sargon.

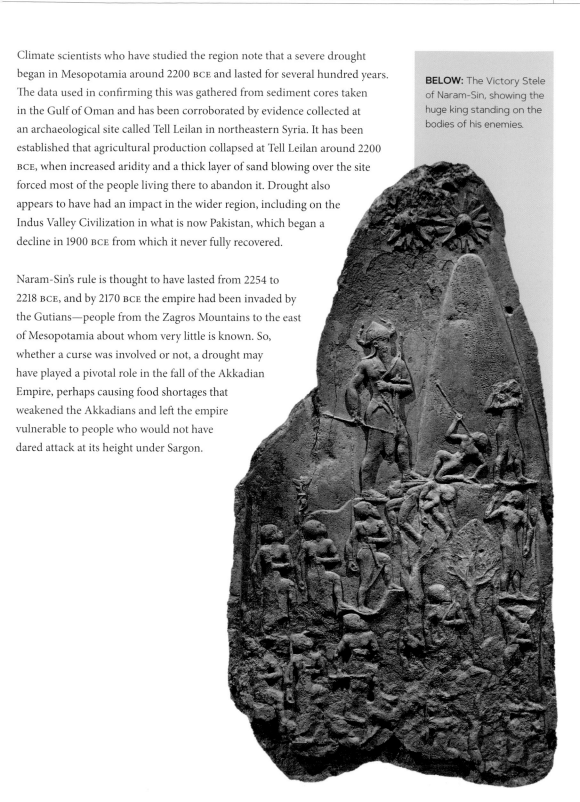

BELOW: The Victory Stele of Naram-Sin, showing the huge king standing on the bodies of his enemies.

What Caused the Collapse of the Hittite Empire?

Where:	Turkey
When:	ca. 1600–ca. 1200 BCE
What:	One of the regional powers of the period
Comment:	The Hittites' demise was part of the Late Bronze Age collapse

ABOVE: Part of a rock relief from Yazılıkaya, a sanctuary near the Hittite capital of Hattusa, showing the 12 Hittite gods of the underworld.

Before archaeological discoveries were made in central Anatolia during the late 19th and early 20th centuries, all that was known about the Hittites came from references to them in the Old Testament of the Bible. Since being rediscovered, it has become clear that they controlled an empire that rivalled that of Egypt, the major regional power of the period, before falling victim to the so-called Late Bronze Age collapse, a fifty-year period beginning around 1200 BCE in which numerous states around the eastern Mediterranean and the Near East fell apart. The entire region entered a dark age from which it took centuries to emerge.

Hattusa

The Hittites are mentioned on numerous occasions in the Bible, where they are said to come from Canaan, which roughly corresponds to the modern-day Levantine coastal region, and from the mountains to the north. Archaeological discoveries made in the latter half of the 19th century included large numbers of inscriptions from the Egyptian and the Assyrian empires, in which a state bearing similarities to that of the biblical Hittites was mentioned, placing them in central Anatolia. The Armana letters, for example, were discovered in the city founded by the pharaoh Akhenaten, the father of Tutankhamen, and included diplomatic correspondence sent to Akhenaten by a king called Suppiluliuma, in which the king expresses the wish that good relations between Egypt and his own kingdom, named as Hatti, should continue into the future.

The Armana letters provided clues to the identity of the Hittites without confirming who they were. The breakthrough came at an archaeological site near the small town of Boğazkale in central Anatolia, where excavations by the German archaeologist Hugo Winckler began in 1906 and have continued sporadically ever since, under the direction of the German Institute of Archaeology. Winckler found what would prove to be the city of Hattusa, the Hatti capital and, though no physical evidence beyond the similarity of the

ABOVE: The Hittite cuneiform alphabet on clay tablets. Cuneiform writing was made by pressing a wedge-shaped reed or stylus into wet clay.

names confirms the identification, it is now widely accepted that the Hatti were the people referred to as the Hittites in the Bible.

As the excavations of Hattusa advanced and further Hittite finds were made across Anatolia, it became apparent that they controlled a major empire that, at its height in the 13th and 14th centuries BCE, encompassed territory occupied by people of different ethnicities and who spoke a variety of different languages. From the Hittite homeland of Hattusa, the empire spread out westward to the Aegean coast of Anatolia and eastward into the Levant and Mesopotamia, where it bordered the Egyptian and Assyrian empires.

Among the extraordinary finds at Hattusa have been the remains of the so-called Great Temple; of massive stone city walls that were 5 miles (8km) long; the gates to the city, including the Lion Gate and the King's Gate; and the acropolis, an upper city containing the royal palace. Perhaps the most remarkable discovery of all has been an enormous archive of inscribed clay tablets that have provided us with detailed information about the Hittite Empire and its dealings with other empires and states in the region. More than

BELOW: The Lion Gate, one of the entrances to Hattusa beyond its monumental stone walls. Towers originally stood on either side of the gate.

20,000 tablets have been found, many inscribed with text in the Hittite language, but some are also written in Akkadian, the language of the Akkadian Empire, which was commonly used in diplomatic communications between states in Mesopotamia and around the eastern Mediterranean.

One of the best-known texts found in the Hittite archive is a copy of a peace treaty agreed between the Hittites and the Egyptians about fifteen years after the Battle of Kadesh, fought in 1274 BCE on the border between the two empires in the Levant. Details of the battle have been found in Egyptian inscriptions and it is now thought to have been the largest chariot battle ever fought, involving more than five thousand chariots. Both sides proclaimed victory, but the fact that the battle resulted in a peace treaty suggests that the outcome was indecisive. The treaty contained an agreement of alliance between the two empires and a promise that, should either suffer an attack by somebody else, the other would come to its aid. It remains the earliest known example of a peace treaty and a copy of it is now displayed on the wall outside the chamber of the United Nations Security Council in New York, providing a reminder that, if the Hittites and Egyptians could settle their differences in a mutually beneficial way, surely it is not beyond us to do the same today.

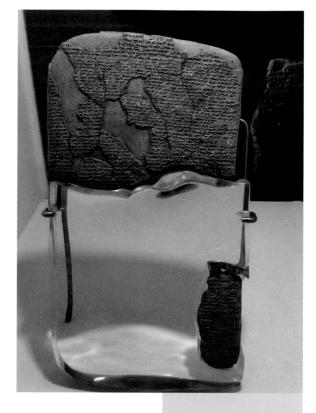

ABOVE: The original Egyptian-Hittite peace treaty, found in Hattusa and now on display in the Museum of the Ancient Orient in Istanbul, Turkey.

The Late Bronze Age Collapse

The Hittite Empire entered into the peace treaty with Egypt around 1260 BCE, suggesting that the two empires were then equally powerful, but only sixty to eighty years afterward, the Hittite Empire fell apart. Archaeologists have found what they describe as a destruction layer in Hattusa, which shows evidence that the city was not simply abandoned and then fell into ruin, but that it suffered some sort of catastrophic event during which its walls were destroyed and its buildings burned down. Similar destruction layers have been found at other Hittite cities across the empire and at numerous other sites around the eastern Mediterranean, all destroyed between 1200 BCE and 1150 BCE. In all, around fifty cities were affected, some never to be occupied again. They

MYCENAEAN GREECE

The Mycenaean civilization developed around 1600 BCE and spread out from the city of Mycenae in the Peloponnese to control most of mainland Greece and the Aegean islands. From around 1250 BCE, fortifications were enlarged in Mycenaean cities, suggesting they were under threat of attack, and during the Late Bronze Age Collapse the state fell apart and many of its cities, including Mycenae, were burned to the ground. The remains of Mycenae were excavated in the late 19th century by Heinrich Schliemann, who discovered the so-called Mask of Agamemnon, a golden funeral mask that Schliemann thought had belonged to Agamemnon, the king of Mycenae in Greek mythology.

RIGHT: The Mask of Agamemnon was found in a burial shaft in Mycenae.

stretched from the Mycenaean city of Pylos in the southern Peloponnese of Greece to Gaza in the southern Levant and as far east as Babylon in southern Mesopotamia. This period of apparent chaos in the region has become known as the Late Bronze Age Collapse and its causes have become the subject of a long-running debate among archaeologists and ancient historians, that shows no sign of being resolved.

The most obvious cause of so much destruction is invasion by hostile forces, but it has never been established who could have carried out such wide-ranging attacks. The destruction occurred some six centuries too early for the Scythians to be implicated and, as many of the destroyed cities were located on the coast, it would appear more likely that they were attacked from the sea. The most commonly expressed theory is that the attackers were the so-called Sea Peoples, often described as being a confederation of people from various locations around the Mediterranean. The major problem with this theory is that it is not backed up with very much evidence and, though some groups have been identified as being part of the Sea Peoples, it is by no means apparent that they would have been capable of inflicting such widespread damage in so many different locations.

The best evidence in support of the Sea Peoples theory comes from a number of relief carvings and inscriptions found in Egypt. These describe attacks on the Egyptians by unidentified people around 1177 BCE. The carvings depict the attackers being accompanied by carts carrying women and children, which is taken to imply that they had not just come to raid Egypt, but intended to settle there. The Egyptians repulsed the attacks and were one of the few people in the eastern Mediterranean not to be greatly affected by the Late Bronze Age Collapse. It is something of a leap, however, to propose that those people defeated by the Egyptians then went on to maraud around the rest of the eastern Mediterranean.

A more likely explanation is that such attacks were part of a broader array of difficulties that came together to affect the region at the same time, perhaps including a dramatic increase in piracy in the Mediterranean, which disrupted trade networks, together with an increase in wars between states and civil unrest within them. There is also evidence of the climate becoming more arid at this time so that, when all of these difficulties are taken together, many of the states across the region were facing a perfect storm of adversity. Whatever the case, the Hittites were among those to fall victim to the collapse and it would be several centuries before the so-called Neo-Hittite states began to arise across Anatolia to fill the power vacuum they left behind them.

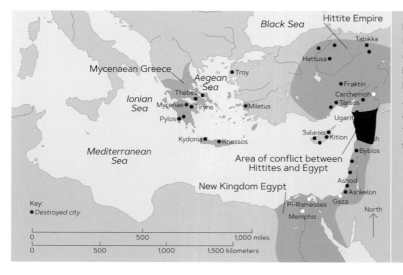

LEFT: The Eastern Mediterranean, showing the contested border region between the Hittites and the Egyptians. The Late Bronze Age Collapse affected almost all of this region, from Pylos in the west to Gaza in the southern Levant.

What Became of the Xiongnu Empire?

Where: Mongolia and northern China

When: ca. 209 BCE–ca. second century CE

What: A confederation of Mongolian tribes

Comment: Reason for end unknown, but perhaps subdued by China

ABOVE: The vast expanses of the steppe grassland of central Mongolia, from which the Xiongnu Empire of Modu Chanyu began to expand.

The Xiongnu were pastoral nomads from the huge expanse of steppe grassland of what is now Mongolia. According to contemporary Chinese sources, once Modu Chanyu became their leader in 209 BCE, he began to establish an extensive empire stretching beyond the boundaries of Mongolia. At its height, the empire included parts of modern-day southern Siberia, eastern Kazakhstan, and northern China, and was considered such a threat by Chinese emperors of the period that an early version of the Great Wall of China was built in an attempt to defend Chinese territory from invasion.

A Steppe Empire

The investigation of the archaeology of the Xiongnu has only really begun in the past few decades and, so far, only a few of the thousands of burial sites identified across Mongolia have been investigated. Even at this early stage it is becoming clear that describing them as being nomadic tribes of the steppe is too simple. Sections of Xiongnu society lived in settled communities, indicating that its vast empire encompassed a complex social structure and included people who were ethnically and linguistically diverse. As work continues, the potential exists for archaeologists to understand the nature of this society in much greater depth than is currently the case. In the meantime, however, we have to rely on Chinese written sources, which, given that the Xiongnu and the Chinese were often in conflict, may not be entirely objective.

ABOVE: A portrait of the ancient Chinese historian Sima Qian. Much of our knowledge of the Xiongnu Empire derives from his work.

One of the principle Chinese sources is the *Records of the Grand Historian* by Sima Qian, who began writing during the early period of the Han dynasty, which held power in China from 202 BCE to 220 CE. The Han succeeded the short-lived Qin dynasty of Qin Shi Huang, now regarded as being the first emperor of China. Qin emerged from the so-called Warring States period as the ruler of a united China and immediately faced conflict with the Xiongnu and other tribal groups on his northern border. Attempts to limit the threat by building a series of walls were only partially successful and, after Qin died in 210 BCE, the dynasty he founded failed to survive. While China entered a period of instability that would see the Han dynasty gain control, Modu Chanyu seized the leadership of the Xiongnu (Chanyu is a title roughly equivalent to emperor). He formed a confederation of tribal peoples and began to expand the territory under his control to build the Xiongnu Empire, exploiting the chaos in China to recapture lands that had previously been taken from the Xiongnu during the Qin dynasty, and then moving into China itself.

This expansion allowed the Xiongnu Empire to control the highly lucrative trade routes across northern China and into central Asia now known as the Silk Road. The loss of these routes, together with almost constant conflict with the Xiongnu in the border region, led the Chinese to mount a full-scale military campaign against the Xiongnu in 129 BCE. This eventually led to the Xiongnu Empire being split in two. The Xiongnu regions along the border became vassal states of China, while other Mongolian tribal groups attacked and conquered those in the north. Around 150 CE, the Xiongnu were only occasionally mentioned in the Chinese sources, for mounting low-level raids across the border—an indication that the empire had come to an end.

Mongolian or Siberian?

An ongoing debate about the Xiongnu concerns their ethnicity and, specifically, if they were originally an indigenous Mongolian people or had migrated to the Mongolian steppe from the west. We know that the Scythians came from southern Siberia and, as well as migrating westward toward Europe,

THE HUN

One disputed theory concerning the fate of the Xiongnu relates how, after the empire was split into two by the Chinese, one half began to move westward across the steppes before eventually arriving in

Eastern Europe, where the people became known as "the Hun." Attila, the king of the Hun from 434–453 CE, became infamous for attacking the Roman Empire and Western Europe. Beyond arriving in Europe from the steppe regions to the east, little is known for certain about the origins of the Hun. They were most likely a mix of many different ethnicities, which could possibly have included a lineage stretching all the way to Mongolia.

LEFT: Detail from *Attila and His Hordes Overrun Italy and the Arts*, painted in 1843 by the French Romantic artist Eugène Delacroix.

they also moved into the Altai Mountains, which span the borders between present-day Russia, Kazakhstan, China, and Mongolia. It is not known if the Scythians, or any other nomadic people, moved further east onto the Mongolian steppe, but the possibility exists that the Xiongnu came from this origin.

Genetic analysis of human remains found in excavated Xiongnu burials tends to support the theory that they were indigenous Mongolians, though DNA markers in about ten percent of the samples tested also showed some European heritage. This suggests that the Xiongnu were of multiple ethnicities, encompassing people from the regions that had been absorbed into their empire, which extended westward as far as the Altai Mountains. The grave goods found in burials exhibit a wide range of artistic styles, also pointing toward a multicultural mix in which the indigenous Mongolian elements of the Xiongnu were influenced by those of others while, no doubt, spreading their own cultural influences as well.

ABOVE: This gold belt buckle from Mongolia dates back to the Xiongnu period. The design of two big cats attacking ibexes betrays Scythian influences.

The Xiongnu Empire was the first of the steppe empires to arise in Mongolia before spreading out into China and central Asia. It preempted a number of later empires that arose and fell across the same region, culminating in the Mongol Empire established in the early 13th century by Genghis Khan, who considered himself to be a descendant of Modu Chanyu. The threat posed by the Mongol Empire led the Chinese to adopt similar measures to defend themselves to those of their predecessors, including building extensive fortified walls across the north of their territory now known collectively as the Great Wall of China. In 1271, Kublai Khan, the grandson of Genghis Khan, established the Yang dynasty, which ruled China until being replaced by the Ming dynasty in 1368, perhaps demonstrating that building border walls does not always achieve the desired results.

What Caused the Kushan Empire to Fall Apart?

Where:	Afghanistan, Central Asia, Pakistan, and India
When:	ca. 30–ca. 375 CE
What:	A multicultural empire that became Buddhist
Comment:	Invaded from all sides; squeezed out

ABOVE: Detail of a third-century Kushan rock relief from northwest Pakistan. It depicts the death of the Buddha on attaining nirvana.

At its height in the first century CE, the Kushan Empire covered an enormous expanse of territory across modern-day Afghanistan and central Asia, which extended southward through Pakistan and into northern India and westward into the northwestern region of China. The Kushans occupied a position at the heart of the Silk Road trade network and were in contact with both the Roman Empire and China. They became very wealthy as a consequence of these trading links, but their empire was relatively short-lived. It began to split apart after around two centuries and, on the death of its last known king in 375 CE, disappeared from the historical record.

The Kushan Expansion

According to early Chinese historical sources, including the *Records of the Grand Historian* by Sima Qian, the Kushans were originally one of the five branches of the Yuezhi, an Indo-European tribal people who inhabited the northern grasslands of what is now the Chinese province of Gansu. Their territory bordered the Mongolian steppes and, during the second century BCE, this brought them into conflict with the expanding Xiongnu Empire, resulting in them being pushed westward to the mountainous Hindu Kush region on the border between Afghanistan and Pakistan. From there, they moved north to settle in Bactria, the region previously occupied by the so-called Greco-Bactrians and which is today where Afghanistan borders Tajikistan and Uzbekistan.

Bactria was the easternmost limit of the Hellenistic world, originally conquered by Alexander the Great and his Macedonian successors, and the Greco-Bactrians were Greek speakers. Once the Kushans had taken over, they absorbed many aspects of Greek culture and adopted the Greek alphabet to develop a writing system for their own Bactrian language. As they expanded in the first century CE, the Kushans took control of central Asian cities on the Silk Road, including Samarkand in Uzbekistan and Merv in Turkmenistan. They also expanded southward along the Indus Valley to dominate the trade routes from the borders of China to the Arabian Sea.

Expansion into the Indian subcontinent brought the region of Pakistan and northern India known collectively as Gandhara under Kushan control and, around 129 CE, the Kushan king Kanishka the Great established Peshawar as the capital city of the empire. At that time, the predominant religion in Gandhara was Buddhism. It was taken up by Kanishka, who went on to promote it across his empire. It is thought that the religion then spread along

THE RABATAK INSCRIPTION

The Rabatak inscription (below) was found in 1993 near the Surkh Kotal archaeological site in the Baghlan province of northern Afghanistan. The site contained buildings dating to the Kushan period and statues of Kushan kings, while the inscription was written during the reign of Kanishka in the Bactrian language spoken by the Kushans. The inscription provides details of the extent of Kanishka's empire and the lineage of Kushan kings, but both the site in which it was found and the Surkh Kotal site were extensively looted during the Afghan civil war in the 1990s and then completely destroyed by the Taliban.

ABOVE: The ruins of the Dharmarajika Stupa in the Kushan city of Taxila. It dates to the second century CE and was once surrounded by Buddhist monasteries.

the Silk Road into China, where the Han dynasty emperors adopted it, and from where it spread further into Southeast Asia. The period of Kanishka's rule, and of the kings who immediately succeeded him, represents the high point of the Kushan Empire, a golden age in which art and architecture flourished. The ruins of Buddhist monasteries and stupas built during this period can still be seen across the region and the surviving Kushan statues of Buddha are now regarded as being some of the finest produced on the Indian subcontinent.

Decline and Rediscovery

The golden age proved to be short-lived because, by the early third century CE, the empire was beginning to come under pressure from all sides, causing it to break up into a number of smaller states. The Persian Empire of the Sassanians captured the Silk Road cities in central Asia and over the following few centuries the Gupta Empire, established by Chandragupta around 319 CE, expanded northward from the Gangetic Plain into Gandhara, bringing the Hindu religion into that region. Further incursions began in the fifth century CE from central Asia by a tribal confederation called the Hephthalites, who are sometimes known as the White Huns, though any relationship between these and the Huns who invaded Europe is disputed. The few remaining Kushan states were no longer able to resist invasion, bringing the last vestiges of the empire to an end.

The Islamic conquests of central Asia, Afghanistan, and the northern region of the Indian subcontinent began in the seventh century, and the spread of Islam from the north led to Buddhism being effectively squeezed out of the region formerly occupied by the Kushan Empire. The Buddhist monasteries and stupas were abandoned and gradually fell into ruin, while many of the statues of Buddha erected during the Kushan golden age were intentionally destroyed due to Islamic objections to any sort of figurative art. As the buildings crumbled away, the Kushan Empire was forgotten and would not be rediscovered for another 1,500 years, when the remaining ruins and artifacts began to be studied in the 19th century.

Among the most remarkable discoveries are the remains of the Kushan city of Taxila, found by the British archaeologist Sir Alexander Cunningham in the 1860s, to the north of Islamabad in what is now the Pakistani province of Punjab. An extensive fortified city known as Sirsukh had been built here during the reign of Kanishka the Great, located at the crossroads of the major trade routes of the period. It became one of the largest cities in the world at that time, with an estimated population of 100,000 inhabitants, but it was lost to the Gupta Empire around 350 CE, before being destroyed by the Hephthalites in the following century. The entire site, which includes ruins from earlier periods as well as from the Kushan Empire, is now a UNESCO World Heritage Site, perhaps indicating that this lost civilization is now in the process of being found.

LEFT: Remaining walls at the UNESCO World Heritage Site of Taxila, one of the largest cities in the world at the time of the Kushan Empire.

What Happened to the Aksumite Empire?

Where: Ethiopia, Eritrea and Djibouti

When: ca. 100–ca. 900 CE

What: An empire built on trade

Comment: Fate unknown, but perhaps a consequence of trade routes moving elsewhere

ABOVE: The Ezana Stone. It was erected in Aksum in about 350 CE to commemorate the expansion of the Aksumite Empire and its conversion to Christianity.

The Aksumite Empire began to grow in prominence around 100 CE due to its position on the East Africa coast of the Red Sea, which allowed it to control a major trade route running from the Indian subcontinent to the Roman Empire. It was centered on the capital city of Aksum, known as Axum today, which is in the state of Tigray in northern Ethiopia. At its height, the empire included most of modern-day Ethiopia, Eritrea, and Djibouti, together with some parts of Sudan, Somalia, Egypt, and the coastal region of Yemen on the other side of the Red Sea, but it went into a long period of decline in the sixth century CE from which it did not recover.

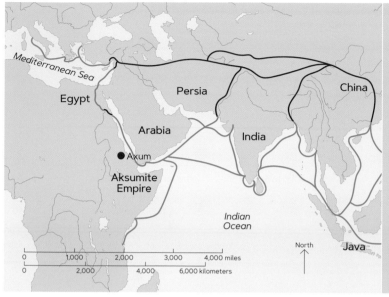

LEFT: The trade routes that brought goods to Europe. The Silk Road is marked in red and the maritime route, which benefited the Aksumite Empire, is in blue.

Maritime Trade

Before the conquest of Egypt by Augustus Caesar in 30 BCE, the principle trading routes between India and the Roman Empire were overland across central Asia, and by sea along the coastline of the Arabian Sea and Persian Gulf. Once Alexandria and other ports on the Egyptian coast had fallen into Roman hands, the route began to switch to a maritime one directly across the Arabian Sea from India to the Red Sea and then on to Egypt. This took considerably less time and goods did not have to pass through as many different states where taxes could be collected. The Aksumite port of Adulis, which is today an archaeological site on the coast of Eritrea, was perfectly placed to control access to the Red Sea by merchant ships carrying cargoes from Indian ports, allowing the empire to levy taxes and engage in its own trade with Rome.

As well as Indian goods, including those from the Kushan Empire, the maritime route carried silks from China and spices from the islands of what is now Indonesia, both of which were highly desirable and expensive in the Roman Empire. Further trading routes ran to Adulis from the African interior and along the east coast of the continent, bringing ivory, gold, exotic animals, and slaves to the Roman Empire. The opportunity to control such highly lucrative trade led to the early Aksumite kings becoming extremely wealthy and, consequently, to their kingdom expanding into the neighboring territory to become an empire.

The city of Aksum became the capital of the empire at some point during this early period and grew in size over the course of the next few centuries. Around 325 CE, the Aksumite emperor Ezana converted to Christianity, an event commemorated on the Ezana Stone, a stele bearing inscriptions in three languages, including the Ge'ez spoken in the Aksumite kingdom, which documents how the conversion occurred. It was erected toward the end of Ezana's reign around 350 CE and can still be seen in modern Axum today. After his conversion, Ezana also began to build churches in Aksum, including the Church of Our Lady Mary of Zion, which has since been rebuilt on the same site on a number of occasions and is said to hold the original Ark of the Covenant.

An Isolated Empire

The exact cause of the decline of the Aksumite Empire is not known, but a primary reason may have been a reduction in the maritime trade between

THE OBELISK OF AXUM

The Obelisk of Axum is one of a number of enormous carved stone pillars erected in the city during the fourth century CE. It was decorated with false doors and windows and is thought to have marked a royal grave. The obelisk is 80ft (24m) tall and weighs around 176 tons (160 tonnes). After the occupation of Ethiopia by the Italian army in 1935, the obelisk was taken to Rome on the orders of Benito Mussolini's fascist regime and erected in the Piazza di Porta Capena. In 2005, after years of diplomatic wrangling, it was returned to Axum and, in 2008, finally reerected in its original position.

LEFT: The Obelisk of Axum, back in its rightful place in the city of Axum after spending fifty years in Rome, Italy.

Europe and India through the Red Sea, resulting from the split in the Roman Empire in 395 CE into the Western Roman Empire and the Byzantine Empire, and the subsequent fall of the Western Roman Empire, conventionally said to have occurred in 479 CE. The Aksumites continued to trade with the Byzantine Empire and enjoyed a second period of prosperity in the early sixth century CE, during the reign of the emperor Kaleb. But a series of wars with the Persian Sassanian Empire in Arabia during the latter part of the sixth century, appears to have put the empire under severe strain, resulting in the loss of its Arabian enclave.

ABOVE: The modern Church of Our Lady Mary of Zion in Axum, built in the 1950s. The original church is thought to have been built in the fifth century CE.

Some historians think that the Plague of Justinian could have afflicted the Aksumite Empire. If this was the case, it would have had a devastating impact. The epidemic was named after the Byzantine emperor Justinian I and is thought to have been an outbreak of bubonic plague that began in Constantinople (now Istanbul), the capital of the Byzantine Empire, around 542 CE. It went on to recur regularly over the following few centuries, causing terrible loss of life in the affected regions.

The rise of Islam on the Arabian peninsula in the early seventh century, followed by the beginning of the Islamic conquests after the death of Muhammad in 632 CE, appears to have disrupted the trade between the two Christian empires of the Byzantines and Aksumites. As Islam spread into North and East Africa, newly constituted caliphates and sultanates took control of the Red Sea so that the Aksumite Empire became increasingly isolated. Little is known about the end of the empire, but an oral tradition tells how a non-Christian princess named Gudit led an attack on Aksum in 960 CE during which the emperor was killed and she took the throne for herself. There is no way of knowing if this story is based on fact and, some time later, a new dynasty called the Zagwe emerged to rule northern Ethiopia. The Aksumite Empire may have fallen away, but it left a lasting legacy of Christianity in Ethiopia and the Ethiopian Orthodox Church, established in the fourth century CE, remains the largest communion in the country.

Why Did the Khmer Empire Decline?

Where:	Cambodia and surrounding areas
When:	802–1434 CE
What:	An empire in Southeast Asia
Comment:	Possibly declined as a consequence of the changing pattern of monsoon rains

ABOVE: Detail of a bas relief from the Bayon, the temple at the center of Angkor Thom, showing a Khmer war elephant and an army going into battle.

At its height in the 12th and 13th centuries, the Khmer Empire ruled over most of the Indochinese peninsula and some of southern China. Angkor, its capital city near the modern Cambodian city of Siem Reap, was the largest city in the world, with a population approaching one million inhabitants. It contained hundreds of monumental stone buildings, including the Angkor Wat temple complex and the walled city of Angkor Thom. During the course of the 14th century, the empire entered into a decline from which it never recovered and the reasons why this happened are not yet fully understood.

The Hydraulic City

The clearest sign of the decline occurred in 1434, when the capital of the Khmer Empire was moved away from Angkor to Phnom Penh. After that time, no further monumental building work was undertaken across the empire and Cambodia entered into what is sometimes called a dark age for the following few centuries. Angkor was not completely abandoned, but the population was severely depleted, with those who remained living in small farming villages. The temples and other monumental buildings became overgrown and forests took root so that the buildings were no longer visible. It was not until the early 20th century that the vegetation began to be cleared and Angkor started to become the tourist destination it is today.

The Khmer King Jayavarman II founded Angkor in 802 and this is sometimes taken as the point at which the Khmer Empire began. The remains of the city demonstrate the extraordinary abilities developed by Khmer stonemasons and also the mastery of the management of water, a necessary requirement because of the region's tropical monsoon climate. Angkor is sometimes referred to as being a "hydraulic city" because of the intricate network of canals, ditches, and reservoirs constructed to channel and store water from the hills to the north, both for use in the city and for the irrigation system required for wetland rice

BELOW: The Bayon temple in Angkor Thom, the compound built within Angkor that served as the last capital city of the Khmer Empire.

production. There was also an extensive drainage system to take excess water out of the city to Tonle Sap Lake to the south. The lake is part of the riverine system of the Mekong Basin, which occupies much of the interior of the Indochinese peninsula. This region is highly prone to flooding during the monsoon season, which lasts from May to October, but the floods also produce highly fertile alluvial soils.

While the most widely admired achievements of the Khmer Empire today are the architectural masterpieces of the temples of Angkor Wat, and a highly developed artistic style demonstrated by its sculpture and bas-relief carvings, the empire owed its success to this hydraulic engineering. The water management system allowed for two or three crops of rice to be grown a year, enough to support the growing population of the city and a large army, which enabled the empire to maintain its grip on its territory and defend itself against outside aggression.

BELOW: The temple of Angkor Wat, reflected in one of the reservoirs built as part of the extensive water-management system of the city.

The Fluctuating Monsoon

One of the more convincing theories explaining this empire's decline suggests that climate change toward the end of the 13th century caused the monsoon to fluctuate between years of intense rain and years of relative drought. Water damage has been observed in Angkor—the result, it is thought, of heavy rainfall in the hills causing major flooding in the city, which overwhelmed the hydraulic system. Developed over the course of centuries, during which time it was enlarged and improved, it is thought that the hydraulic system suffered sudden damage by floods that could not be repaired in time before more flooding occurred in the following year. The impact of floods and droughts on the production of rice could have been even more serious, making it impossible to grow enough of the empire's staple food to maintain such a large population.

In recent years, citing climate change as responsible for the collapse of past civilizations has become something of a trend. In the case of the Khmer Empire though, climate change really does appear to have played a part in the decline. However, as with other lost civilizations, it is most likely to have been just one part of a complex array of problems that came together to undermine the empire, rather than being the primary cause.

The political system of the Khmer Empire relied on the leadership of a hereditary absolute monarch, and, like many other states with similar systems, it became unstable when a succession was contested or if a new king proved to be less capable than their predecessor. There was also a religious divide in Khmer society between Buddhists and Hindus, and, though there are plenty of examples of successful multifaith societies, modern history demonstrates how some such societies can unravel. Another factor was the regular incidence of conflict with Thailand, including in 1432 when the Thais captured and looted Angkor, which must surely have contributed to the empire's decline. Altogether, there are a multitude of reasons why the Khmer Empire came to an end, no doubt some completely unknown to us now.

THE GREAT PLAGUE

It is not known if the Great Plague, or the Black Death as it was known in Europe, reached Cambodia. It was recorded in China in the early 1330s, so outbreaks in Southeast Asia may well have occurred around that time. The impact of plague could be devastating; during some outbreaks, more than half the population died. Other infectious diseases such as cholera and smallpox may also have been present. The effect of an epidemic in addition to a drought and flooding caused by climate change could have caused insurmountable problems from which the Khmer Empire was unable to recover.

What Became of the Ghurid Sultanate?

Where:	Centered on Ghor province, Afghanistan
When:	1146–1215 CE
What:	A short-lived Afghan empire
Comment:	Sultanate was broken up due to the absence of a male heir

ABOVE: The Qutb Minar, a minaret in Delhi, India, originally erected in 1193 by Quṭb al-Din Aibak after the city was captured by the Ghurid Sultanate.

The short-lived Ghurid Sultanate was originally centered on the city of Firozkoh in the Ghor province of what is now central Afghanistan. At its height, it encompassed a huge territory, stretching for 2,000 miles (3,200km) from the region of Khorasan in eastern Iran to Bengal in the east of the Indian subcontinent. It may only have lasted some seventy years and is hardly remembered at all today, but it played an important role in the spread of Islam into northern India before falling apart and being replaced in the subcontinent by the much longer-lasting Delhi Sultanate of the Mamluks.

The Rise of the Ghurids

The exact heritage of the Ghurid dynasty is not known for certain. It was most likely of Iranian descent and may have been started by provincial governors in one of the numerous offshoots of the Persian Empire, which ruled the Khorasan and Ghor regions during what is known as the Iranian Intermezzo. Their immediate predecessor in Ghor was the Ghaznavid dynasty, a Turkic people of central Asian origin who were originally Mamluks, enslaved soldiers, and bodyguards of the Arabic sultanates that had arisen during the period of the Islamic conquests.

At some point, the Ghaznavid dynasty became assimilated with Persian culture, speaking the Persian language and converting to the Islamic faith. After capturing Ghor province in 1011, the Ghaznavids converted what had previously been a predominantly Buddhist region to Islam and ruled their empire—which included most of modern-day Afghanistan and some parts of Pakistan—from their capital city of Ghazni in the east of Afghanistan. As their empire expanded into Persia, central Asia, and further into the Indian subcontinent, they appear to have left the remote and isolated province of Ghor to be governed by members of the Ghurid dynasty. In 1146, and with the Ghaznavids occupied with fighting among themselves and defending the

BELOW: The ornate pillars of the Quwwat-ul-Islam Mosque in Delhi, part of the complex built by Quṭb al-Din Aibak, who later established the Delhi Sultanate.

THE MINARET OF JAM

The Minaret of Jam, in Ghor province, is one of the few remaining examples of architecture from the period of Ghurid dynasty. Thought to have been erected in the 1190s by one of the Ghurid sultans, it is 213ft (65m) tall. It is constructed of brick and decorated with Islamic geometric designs, together with a Kufic inscription in turquoise tiles. The minaret is thought to mark the location of the lost city of Firozkoh, but, although the ruins of a number of buildings are known to be in the vicinity of the minaret, this claim has yet to be fully investigated and, in recent years, the site has been extensively damaged by looters.

LEFT: The Minaret of Jam clearly inspired the design of the Qutb Minar in Delhi and many other Islamic buildings across the Indian subcontinent.

borders of their empire, the Ghurids rose up against their overlords, taking control of Ghor and establishing their capital at Firozkoh. The head of the dynasty during this early period of self rule was Sayf al-Din Sur, who began to call himself "sultan" and to expand the area of his fledgling empire by attacking the Ghaznavids to his east and the Seljuk dynasty in Khorasan to the west.

In 1149, Sayf was succeeded by his younger brother Ala al-Din Husayn and during his reign the empire expanded further as he won victories against the Ghaznavids in what appears to have become a personal vendetta after the Ghaznavid sultan was implicated in the murder of another brother of the Ghurid dynasty. Over the course of the following decades, the Ghurids took the Ghaznavid capital and then cities of Multan and Lahore in Pakistan, which effectively brought the Ghaznavid Empire to an end.

In 1186, after capturing Lahore under the leadership of Mu'izz ad-Din Muhammad, better known as Muhammad of Ghor, the Ghurid Sultanate, as it could now reasonably be called, moved farther southward into Punjab, Rajasthan, and Gujarat, where it defeated the Hindu rulers of these regions in a series of huge battles reputed to have involved hundreds of thousands of men. In 1193, Muhammad captured Delhi and installed one of his Mamluk generals, Quṭb al-Din Aibak, as governor of the city before continuing eastward to take territory all the way to Bengal in what is today Bangladesh.

Muhammad of Ghor

The Ghurid Sultanate reached its pinnacle under Muhammad of Ghor's rule, and he is now considered to have been instrumental in bringing Islam into northern India. He was assassinated in 1206, near the town of Sohawa in the Punjab region of Pakistan, where his tomb can now be found. He was traveling back to Afghanistan from India and the identity of his assailants is not known, but they may have been members of one of the remaining Hindu tribes of Punjab who had not converted to Islam.

Muhammad left no male heir. On his death, the sultanate entered into a period of confusion and infighting. In the ensuing chaos, it proved impossible for one sultan to take control of such a large empire, so it was divided between the high-ranking Mamluk officers of Muhammad's army. Quṭb al-Din Aibak became the first Sultan of Delhi and established a Mamluk dynasty that expanded the Delhi Sultanate over the northern part of the Indian subcontinent. Subsequent dynasties captured much of the remaining Indian subcontinent, until the Delhi Sultanate itself fell to the Mughal Empire, in 1526. During both the Delhi Sultanate and the Mughal Empire, the ruling elites continued to follow Persian and Islamic culture, maintaining Persian as the official language of court proceedings right up until 1857, at which point the Mughal Empire was formally dissolved by the British and it became part of the British Raj.

The last of the Ghurid dynasty was overthrown in 1215, when Ghor was attacked from the west and seized by the Khwarazmian dynasty, who had expanded out of Khorasan. Theirs would prove to be a short-lived victory; seven years later, the Mongol army of Genghis Khan invaded Ghor, destroying the former Ghurid capital city of Firozkoh to such an extent that it was effectively wiped off the map. Over time, the location of the city was forgotten and, had it not been for the exploits of Muhammad of Ghor in northern India, the memory of the Ghurid Sultanate as a whole may have been lost as well.

Norse Settlements

Ancestral Puebloans   Cahokia
                                ● ● Roanoke Island

Maya Civilization

● Easter Island

Chapter Four
POST-CLASSICAL DISAPPEARANCES

The civilizations featured in this chapter are those that have
disappeared in more recent times. We start with the collapse
of the Maya civilization of central America around 900 CE and
move on to survey lost civilizations in Greenland, North America,
and Easter Island in the Pacific Ocean, before finally discussing
the so-called Lost Colony of Roanoke Island.

What Precipitated the Collapse of the Classic Maya Civilization?

Where: Mexico, Guatemala, and Belize

When: ca. 250–ca. 900 CE

What: An advanced civilization of city-states

Comment: Several factors caused the collapse, likely including an extended drought

ABOVE: This detail of a characteristic Maya bas-relief carving shows a Maya king wearing a ceremonial headdress and carrying an ornately carved staff.

The Maya civilization developed on the lowlands of the Yucatán Peninsula and the interior highlands of modern-day southern Mexico, Guatemala, and Belize. During its classical period, from 250 to 900 CE, the cities of the southern lowlands region expanded and numerous monumental stone buildings such as pyramids and temples were built. Toward the end of the classical period, civilization in the southern lowlands collapsed, while the northern lowlands and highlands were much less affected. The causes of this collapse have been vigorously debated since the rediscovery of these sites began in the 19th century.

Collapse in the Southern Lowlands

Approximately six million people of Maya ethnicity still inhabit this region, so it would be rather ridiculous to describe them as survivors of a societal collapse that occurred more than a thousand years ago. Nevertheless, something happened across the southern lowlands between 800 and 900 CE, which caused the well-established Maya cites of Tikal and Calakmul to become almost completely abandoned, and the surrounding villages to become so depopulated that, afterward, only around ten percent of the previous population remained.

One possible cause of the collapse was the high incidence of warfare between rival cities. The Maya were never a unified nation under a single leader but, like the ancient Greeks, belonged to numerous city-states. Just as Athens and Sparta were regularly in conflict, Tikal and Calakmul rivaled one another and low-level raiding could sometimes escalate into full-scale war. Evidence of the impact of violent conflict can be found at Aguateca, a city in the southern lowlands that was attacked by unknown assailants around 800 CE. Archaeologists have found numerous personal possessions in the city, indicating that it was abandoned so quickly that people did not have the time to gather such items before they left. Many of the buildings were burned down,

BELOW: The Great Plaza at the center of Tikal, one of the cities of the southern lowlands, which declined after 900 CE before being abandoned.

LEFT: A stone stela, or commemorative pillar, in the Main Plaza at the center of Aguateca. In about 800 CE, the city was attacked and then abandoned by its inhabitants.

giving the impression that the attackers intended to destroy the city rather than mount a raid to capture it or to take prisoners—a common feature of Maya raids, which sought to provide the victims needed for religious rituals involving human sacrifice.

Defensive walls had been erected in Aguateca shortly before it was destroyed, suggesting that the attack was not unexpected, and that it could have been just one incident in a wider outbreak of war. But, as devastating as it apparently was for Aguateca, there is little evidence that other cities suffered a similar fate around the same time. If war between cities played a role in the overall collapse, then it more likely had an indirect affect whereby resources became depleted and vital activities such as farming and trade were disrupted.

As well as fighting each other, the Maya were also sometimes at war with the Toltecs, who occupied the territory immediately to the north, and with the powerful city-state of Teotihuacan in central Mexico. But most of

THE TOLTECS

The Toltec Empire occupied territory to the north of the Maya city-states, centered on the capital city of Tula, which is some 45 miles (70km) to the north of Mexico City. The empire arose during the sixth century and had a long trading relationship with the Maya, but it is not clear if the Toltecs played any role in their collapse. Similarities between the architecture of Tula and Chichén Itzá have led to suggestions that the Toltecs took control over the city after the collapse in the southern lowlands, but it is just as likely that such similarities arose through a long process of peaceful cultural exchange as a consequence of the trading links.

the time, the Maya engaged in trading relationships with these states and, aside from the disruption caused by the occasional conflict, there is no reason to suppose that an attack from either of these, or from any other outside forces, could have been responsible for the collapse.

It would also appear unlikely for an epidemic disease to have been responsible, though the high population densities in the southern lowlands would have ensured the rapid spread of an infectious disease, resulting in a high number of casualties. The terrible consequences of diseases such as smallpox on the indigenous peoples of the Americas in the aftermath of European colonization demonstrated how devastating epidemics could be, but the Maya states in the northern lowlands and the highlands did not collapse and, had an epidemic occurred, it would surely have spread to those regions as well.

The Drought Theory

In recent years, research has shown that a prolonged drought across the region inhabited by the Maya began around 800 CE, and this is thought to have had a greater impact in the southern lowlands than anywhere else. In 2018, a study was published in which deposits of gypsum in the sediment at the bottom of a lake in the southern lowlands were examined. Lake sediments are laid down in an annual cycle, forming layers that can be dated, and the gypsum in these sediments crystallizes during this process. Water remaining within the gypsum

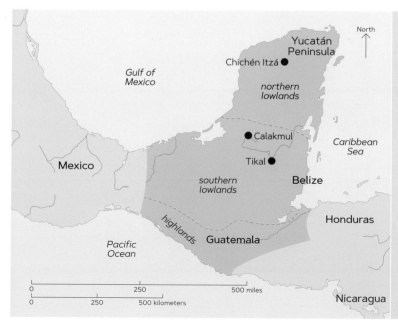

LEFT: The territory occupied by the Maya civilization in present-day Mexico, Guatemala, and Belize. The southern lowlands of the empire are located at the base of the Yucatán Peninsula.

can be dated and, since the chemical composition of lake water has been shown to vary depending on the amount of rainfall, analyzing this water allows scientists to determine how much rain has fallen in any particular year.

What the research on the lake sediments found was that annual rainfall from 800 to 900 CE was between 40–70 percent lower than it had been in previous years, confirming the occurrence of a serious and persistent drought throughout the period in which the collapse took place. The Maya in the northern lowlands and the highlands must also have experienced this drought, but there are reasons why the southern lowlands were more seriously affected by it. For example, the city-states in this region were much more reliant on rainwater for farming and domestic use, because they had access to fewer naturally occurring sources of groundwater than city-states in other regions. At Tikal, there were no permanent groundwater sources at all, so a city with a population of up to eighty thousand people at its height was completely dependent on rainfall, making it highly vulnerable to water shortages when drought struck.

In the early part of the classical period, the populations of the cities in the southern lowlands increased rapidly, so farming had to become more intensive to supply enough food for the people living there. As the cities expanded, each

BELOW: Two jaguar heads at the base of a staircase in Chichén Itzá, the Maya city that persisted for centuries after Tikal and Calakmul had been abandoned.

developed a water-management system that involved the large-scale storage of rainwater. The climate was relatively stable during this period, and each system was capable of supplying enough water for intensive farming. Even without a water shortage, Maya farming methods may have become unsustainable over time because pests and diseases build up rapidly in tropical regions and tropical soils can quickly become depleted of nutrients after the trees have been cleared. If water stress becomes a feature too, as it must have done in the southern lowlands, then there is a high likelihood that the farming will fail. In such circumstances, people face the choice of moving away or starving.

ABOVE: Maya culture is alive and well today, as we can see from this Guatemalan woman weaving textiles on a traditional Mayan backstrap loom.

While Tikal and Calakmul were becoming depopulated, the city of Chichén Itzá situated in the northern lowlands continued to thrive. The limestone geology in this region means that underground supplies of water can be accessed through so-called cenotes, naturally occurring sinkholes through the surface rock, so the people of Chichén Itzá would not have experienced the same levels of water shortage during the drought. Even so, by around 1200, this city also went into decline and, though it was probably not completely abandoned by the time of the Spanish conquest in the early 16th century, by then it was no longer the major urban and religious center it had been at its height. The reasons for Chichén Itzá's decline are not clear, but when the Spanish arrived, they found numerous smaller Maya settlements and a thriving economy in the northern lowlands, suggesting that Maya society had not really collapsed at all. People had adapted to changing circumstances and were beginning to live their lives in ways that did not involve inhabiting large cities or constructing monumental stone buildings. Our inference now, that the Maya somehow became less civilized because they no longer lived in cities, is perhaps a consequence of our preference for urban living rather than a reflection of Maya societies of the past.

What Made the Ancestral Puebloans Leave?

Where:	Southwest North America
When:	ca. 750–ca. 1300 CE
What:	Native American people from the Four Corners region
Comment:	Reasons for dispersal unknown, but perhaps because of drought

The Ancestral Puebloans lived in a region of the North American Southwest now known as the Four Corners and named for the point on the map were the states of Utah, Colorado, New Mexico, and Arizona meet. This distinctive culture arose some time around 750 CE and archaeological remains of their buildings exist across the region today, notably in Mesa Verde and Chaco Canyon. Cliff houses, built under the rock overhangs of canyon walls, are perhaps now the best known of their buildings, which also included so-called Great Houses and circular ceremonial spaces known as *kivas*. By around 1300, the Ancestral Puebloans had moved away from the area and they never returned.

ABOVE: An Ancestral Puebloan black-and-white-ware pitcher, with a characteristic geometric pattern and unusual handle in the shape of a jaguar.

The Cliff Houses

Owing to the dry climate of the Four Corners, the buildings and artifacts left behind by the Ancestral Puebloans some 700 years ago remain in remarkably good condition. Archaeologists have found corncobs and black-and-white Ancient Puebloan pottery in the cliff houses. Wooden beams have allowed scientists to date the houses using dendrochronology, which shows that the houses were built less than one hundred years before the Ancestral Puebloans left the region. In some cases the houses were just decades old, suggesting that such construction methods may have been a response to an increasing level of threat in the years before people started leaving the area.

The Ancestral Puebloans had been living in this region for six hundred years before they began to build the cliff houses. Their culture is thought to have developed from the so-called Basketmaker culture, named because archaeological sites from this period usually contain lots of baskets. It had existed in the region for at least 1,500 years and may itself have developed from previous cultures going back for thousands of years. In order to have lived in the region for so long, these cultures must have been well adapted to the environment and the challenges it presented, so their reasons for leaving must have been significant.

Before they began to construct the cliff houses, the Ancestral Puebloans lived in settled villages in open locations on the tops of mesas and in canyons. The Great Houses they built featured hundreds of rooms spread out over three or

LEFT: The ruins of an Ancestral Puebloan Great House in Chaco Canyon, New Mexico. The Great Houses could accommodate hundreds of people.

LEFT: Cliff Palace in Mesa Verde. After living in the open for generations, around 1190 CE, the Ancestral Puebloans moved to houses built into cliff faces.

four stories in which generations of extended families all lived together. They were farmers, growing crops of corn, beans, and squash, and used river water and stored rainwater to irrigate their crops. Having lived in this way for generations, they then began to build the cliff houses, which were only accessible using wooden ladders and ropes. These new settlements varied in size from as few as one or two houses to sites such as Cliff Palace in Mesa Verde, where more than one hundred dwellings are clustered together to form what looks like a group of apartment blocks wedged under a cliff.

One theory as to why the Ancestral Puebloans began to live in these cliff houses, and then vacated the area completely, is that they came under attack from other Native American people who had moved into the area. Some archaeological evidence supports this idea, even though the Ancestral Puebloans had lived alongside the Navajo people for hundreds of years albeit with strained relations at times. An alternative idea is that different bands of Ancestral Puebloans began to fight with each other after a prolonged drought took hold across the American Southwest. Farming in this region is a marginal activity at the best of times and it may have been that the agricultural system that had developed during the previous wetter period could no longer support so many people once the climate became drier, prompting violent competition between different villages as they attempted to secure the available resources.

The Living Descendants

When the archaeological sites in the Four Corners region were first investigated, in the 1920s, the fate of the people who had lived in the cliff houses was not known and was considered to be something of a mystery. They became known as the Anasazi, a name given to them by the Navajo, although in recent years this name has fallen into disuse following objections raised by living descendants because it means "ancient enemies." Among these descendants are the Pueblo people, who acquired their name during the period of Spanish rule because they lived in towns and villages (pueblo is Spanish for village), and they have settled on the name of the Ancestral Puebloans for their forbears.

A cluster of Pueblo villages can be found today along the Rio Grande to the north of Albuquerque, New Mexico, and the people here have maintained many aspects of their culture despite the intrusions they have faced over the years. They think that their ancestors moved away from the Four Corner simply because it made sense to do so, whatever the reason may have been. In Native American societies in general, it was by no means unusual for communities to make a collective decision to move elsewhere and, in the case of the Ancestral Puebloans, that decision may have been due to a desire to relocate to an area where the living was easier, as much as it was a consequence of drought or violence in their home territory. It could be, therefore, that they were drawn to their new home rather than being forced out of their old one, in which case archaeologists studying the ancient cliff houses in the Four Corners in an attempt to discover why the Ancestral Puebloans left the area are looking in the wrong place.

THE HOPI

The Hopi are descendants of the Ancestral Puebloans and many of them still live on the Hopi Reservation in northeastern Arizona, known as Hopitutskwa by the Hopi people, and surrounded by the much larger Navajo Nation. According to the Hopi website, Hopitutskwa consists of twelve villages located on the tops of three mesas and, while many people now live in modern houses, a few of the traditional stone houses are still occupied. They also maintain their traditional culture, including the Hopi language, and farm corn, beans, and squash as their ancestors used to do.

BELOW: The adobe houses of Taos Pueblo, New Mexico, one of the places where the Ancestral Puebloans settled after migrating away from the Four Corners.

What Happened to the Greenland Norse?

Where:	Greenland
When:	Late 10th–early 15th century
What:	Norse settlements in Greenland
Comment:	A colder climate and numerous other difficulties made the settlements unsustainable

ABOVE: Erik the Red, shown in the frontispiece from a 1688 edition of *Gronlandia (Greenland)* by the Icelandic scholar Arngrímur Jónsson.

According to the Icelandic sagas, composed some three centuries after the event, the Norse settlements on Greenland were first established in 985 CE by Erik the Red—a date that roughly corresponds with the one determined by archaeologists. The settlements maintained contact with Iceland and Norway for more than four centuries before going silent in the early 15th century. Since archaeologists began studying the Norse ruins that remain in Greenland, various theories have been put forward to explain the fate of the Greenland Norse. So far no definitive answer has been found.

The Edge of the Known World

The Norse established two main settlements on Greenland: the Eastern Settlement on the southwestern tip of the island, and the Western Settlement on a fjord farther north along the coast. The ruins of the Western Settlement can be found inland from Nuuk, the capital city of Greenland today. At their height, the Norse settlements numbered around 2,500 people, living on farmsteads scattered around churches, several ruins of which can still be seen today. In 1124, a bishop was sent to Greenland from Norway and a cathedral was built at Garðar in the Eastern Settlement. The stone foundations are all that remain of the cathedral, though remnants of the walls of the bishop's house are still standing. The best-preserved ruins are of Hvalsey Church, also in the Eastern Settlement, where the solidly built walls and gable ends of the small building have so far resisted the weather and remain standing near the head of a fjord.

The Norse people of the Greenland settlements may have been living at the extreme edge of the known world as far as Europe was concerned, but they maintained a regular trading relationship with Iceland, making the trip of 900 miles (1500km) by ship in around two weeks. The most lucrative trade was in

ABOVE: The ruins of Hvalsey Church, one of 16 churches built by the Greenland Norse in the Eastern Settlement to serve about 400 farms.

walrus ivory, a highly sought-after commodity in northern Europe in the early medieval period because the trade in elephant ivory from the African continent and from India had been interrupted by the Islamic conquests in the Middle East and North Africa. During the summer months, the Greenland Norse embarked on seasonal walrus hunts to Disko Bay in northern Greenland and traded the walrus ivory in Iceland for iron tools, cooking pots, timber for

VINLAND

After relating stories about the exploits of Erik the Red, the Icelandic sagas go on to describe how his son, Leif Erikson, traveled west from Greenland to establish the settlement of Vinland. If this was the case, then he arrived on the North American continent almost five hundred years before Christopher Columbus landed there. In 1960, a Norse archaeological site dating to around 1000 CE was found at L'Anse aux Meadows on the northern tip of the island of Newfoundland. The site is thought to have been a base from which Norse sailors explored farther south and, as no other confirmed Norse sites have been found in North America, it currently marks the farthest known westward point reached by the Norse.

BELOW: An aerial view of L'Anse aux Meadows.

boatbuilding, and other essentials not otherwise available in Greenland. Beyond such traded items, they had to be self-sufficient, raising cattle and sheep, growing barley, and hunting for seals and caribou. Even in the best of years, it must have been a hard life of long and bitterly cold winters and very short summers, but the Greenland Norse had come from Iceland and Norway in the first place, where conditions were not very much different; aside from the remoteness of their outpost, their way of life was probably quite similar.

The last written source concerning the Greenland Norse was a letter about a marriage held at Hvalsey Church in 1408, the details of which were noted in Icelandic historical records. Some time shortly after that, all contact was lost, until the early 1720s, when the Danish missionary Hans Egede sailed to Greenland to look for the settlements with the intention of converting the people he found there to protestantism. What he actually found were the remains of deserted settlements and long-abandoned buildings, leading him to speculate that the inhabitants had been attacked by the Inuit, who had arrived in southern Greenland about a century after the Norse, or had succumbed to the climate and had exhausted the soil essential for farming.

ABOVE: Hans Egede, painted in 1745 by the Danish artist Johan Hörner. In the 1720s, Egede found the abandoned Norse settlements on Greenland.

In more recent times, archaeologists have established that the Western Settlement was abandoned around 1350, while the Eastern Settlement carried on for around seventy years longer. The couple who were married in Hvalsey Church were recorded as living in Iceland in the late 1420s, so it is possible that the rest of the Greenland Norse had also left for an easier life elsewhere, though the lack of records of such a migration in Iceland and Norway suggests that this is unlikely to have been the case. The fact that nobody in either country appears to have known that the settlements had been abandoned also indicates that a mass exodus did not take place, though the possibility remains that people began to leave in small numbers over a long period of time so that their arrival in Iceland was not considered worthy of note.

A Refusal to Adapt?

Until recently, the prevailing theory among archaeologists was that the Greenland Norse had not fully adapted to life in the extreme conditions they encountered. They first arrived in Greenland during the so-called Medieval Warm Period, a time during which the climate of Europe and around the

North Atlantic was relatively mild, and this allowed them to set up farms and to maintain contact with Iceland and Norway. This lasted from around 950 to 1250, after which the climate began to grow considerably colder so that, in Europe, the period from around 1350 to the 19th century has become known as the Little Ice Age. As the climate grew colder in Greenland, established farming methods became less sustainable and, according to the theory at least, the Norse people were not prepared to change their way of life when faced with such difficult circumstances. They refused to adopt the hunting and fishing lifestyle of the Inuit people who had moved to southern Greenland, instead persisting with the same farming methods, which degraded the soil until it was completely exhausted.

The problem with this theory is that it is not supported by the work carried out on the Norse settlements by archaeologists over the past few decades. Excavations of middens, as archaeologists call rubbish heaps, found near farmsteads, have found plenty of evidence that the Greenland Norse hunted seals, whales, and other marine life for food, as well as walrus for ivory, while investigations of the fields around the farmsteads have shown that they managed their land in such a way as to maintain soil fertility. They did, after all, persist in Greenland for more than four centuries; had they been poor farmers, this surely would not have been possible.

ABOVE: The rugged landscape of Greenland, a challenging environment for farming at the best of times, was perhaps impossible during the Little Ice Age.

The latest research has led to more nuanced theories as to what happened to the Greenland Norse. These take into account the impact of an increasingly cold climate on farming, but also consider the possibility that other factors were involved in the peoples' demise. As the climate grew colder, increasing quantities of pack ice in the North Atlantic would have made walrus-hunting expeditions and the passage to Iceland more difficult and dangerous. The climate data from the period also shows an increase in the number and severity of storms in the region, exacerbating the problem and potentially leading to the Greenland Norse becoming even more isolated. At the same time, the Portuguese were beginning to establish new maritime trade routes to Africa, which allowed elephant ivory to be imported into Europe again and, as elephant ivory was considered superior to walrus ivory, this must have significantly reduced the demand for the most lucrative commodity traded by the Greenland Norse.

In the 1350s, the Black Death spread to Norway and then to Iceland. While we don't know if the disease reached Greenland, half the population of Iceland perished at this time, which must surely have been a factor in the loss of contact between the two regions. In any event, at some time around 1410 or 1420, no more ships arrived in Iceland from Greenland and it appears that nobody set out from Iceland to find out why their trading partners had gone silent. We may never know for certain what happened, but it is not hard to envisage that, with the Norse settlements facing severe difficulties on all sides, and having become completely cut off, they may simply have died out. Or perhaps the remaining people decided that enough was enough and left their homes for Iceland, only to be lost at sea in a storm.

BELOW: A queen from the 12th-century Lewis chessmen, found on the Scottish island of Lewis and made from walrus ivory, possibly from Greenland.

Why Were Cahokia and Its Mounds Abandoned?

Where:	Illinois, USA
When:	ca. 1050–ca. 1300 CE
What:	A pre-Columbian Native American city
Comment:	Possibly abandoned because of a cooling climate

ABOVE: Monk's Mound, the largest of the Cahokia earth mounds. It was originally a pyramid, but has spread out as the earth has settled.

Cahokia is an archaeological site just outside Collinsville, Illinois, which is on the eastern side of the Mississippi River directly opposite St. Louis. The site is composed of some eighty mounds built by people of the Mississippian culture, a Native American civilization that flourished throughout much of the Mississippi valley before the first Spanish exploration of the region in the 16th century. Archaeologists think that Cahokia was the largest settlement and possibly the center of the culture, a city with a population approaching 30,000 inhabitants at its height, and which developed incredibly rapidly around 1050 CE before declining for unknown reasons during the 13th century.

The Mounds

The Cahokia Mounds, as the site is now called, was originally named in the 17th century after the Cahokia, the Native American people who were living in the area when it was first visited by French explorers. It is not known if the Cahokia were related to the people who were living at the site when it was at its height in the 11th and 12th centuries, or what the Native American name for it may have been. It was originally considerably larger than it is today, being composed of perhaps as many as 120 mounds, but before it was given protected status in the 1960s, some of the mounds had been flattened and roads had been built through the site. More mounds are known to have existed at other nearby sites on either side of the Mississippi River, but almost all of these have been lost during the urban development of St. Louis and East St. Louis.

Cahokia is thought originally to have been a relatively modest sacred site that, around 1050, suddenly exploded in size. Monk's Mound, the largest of the mounds, also appears to have been one of the earliest, built in stages and beginning before the rest of the site was developed. Like the other mounds,

BELOW: An aerial view of the Cahokia mounds site, looking across to Monk's Mound and the Mississippi River in the distance.

it was built using earth and clay thought to have been transported to the site by hand in baskets, and it was built up and enlarged on a number of occasions. A ramp with stairs made from wooden logs led to a platform at the top, where a wooden temple stood. It is now 100ft (30m) tall, but as the earth has settled and spread over the years, it would have been much taller originally. Even so, the view from the top across to St. Louis and the so-called American Bottom—the flat floodplain of the Mississippi River—is spectacular and allowed the Mound Builders an opportunity to survey their entire domain.

Cahokia is the largest site constructed during the period of the Mississippian culture and there are around ten other, smaller, sites where mounds were built. The reason why so many mounds were built here is not known, but the few that have been excavated have contained burials of what may have been a tribal chief together with others, some of which appear to have been sacrificial victims. It is also currently not known why Cahokia underwent such a rapid period of expansion, though it has been noted that this coincided with the onset of the Medieval Warm Period. One theory suggests that the warm weather led to an increase in agricultural productivity based on the cultivation of corn and this caused a rapid growth in population across what may have been a confederation of people of the Mississippian culture, all of whom held the Cahokia site to be sacred. Whatever the case, Cahokia expanded around Monk's Mound to cover a huge area, the full extent of which is only just becoming apparent as archaeologists continue to investigate the site.

ABOVE: A typical Mississippian culture bowl, found at Cahokia and now in the site's museum. It is filled with corn, a staple food of the culture.

Abandoned

The reason for the decline and subsequent abandonment of Cahokia around 1300 are, like so much to do with the Mississippian culture, not well understood. If population growth in the first place was a consequence of the Medieval Warm Period and its impact on agricultural production, then the Little Ice Age that followed may well have led to the farming system coming under stress. But the alluvial soils in the American Bottom are some of the most fertile in America; even if farming became more difficult, the cold snap is unlikely to have brought it to a complete standstill. It may therefore have led to a reduction in the site rather than its complete abandonment.

Another possibility is that Cahokia became uninhabitable in the wake of a huge flood much like the one experienced in the Mississippi valley in 2011, though such an event would surely have left archaeological evidence at the site. In any case, people had been living near the river for hundreds of years before the site was abandoned, so they would have been used to floods and would have developed ways to deal with them. There is also no substantial archaeological evidence of any large-scale warfare or civil unrest beyond what appears to have been the construction of a defensive stockade around the site toward the end of its use. The truth is that we simply don't know why people moved away from Cahokia or where they went, but it is possible that further light will be shed on this mystery in the years to come as the archaeological investigation continues at the site, and at other sites constructed by the Mississippian culture in the region.

THE VACANT QUARTER

A huge swath of territory around the Cahokia site remains lacking in archaeological sites and artifacts that can be dated to later than 1450. This includes the Mississippi and Ohio valleys down to the confluence of the two rivers. Archaeologists refer to this area as the Vacant Quarter and it appears to have become depopulated before the 1530s, when the Spanish explorer Hernando de Soto traveled through it. This suggests that the depopulation was not the result of epidemic disease spread by European colonialism that devastated so many other Native American societies. But, as yet, no other convincing explanation has been found.

RIGHT: Hernando de Soto.

What Befell the Indigenous People of Easter Island?

Where: Easter Island, southeast Pacific

When: ca. 1200–present

What: Collapse of the indigenous people

Comment: Declined due to environmental degradation, then collapsed after European contact

ABOVE: A rock-cut image of the Easter Island god Makemake and the islet of Motu Nui, where tern's eggs were collected as part of the birdman cult.

Easter Island, or Rapa Nui, as it is known in the Polynesian language of its inhabitants, is famous around the world for its monumental stone statues known as moai. It is also known for what has been described by some archaeologists as a societal collapse during the 16th century, before it was first visited by Europeans, brought on by the overexploitation of the environment as a consequence of large increases in population. It is often used as an example of what can happen when environmental degradation is allowed to continue unchecked, but in recent years this version of events on the island has come into question.

The Moai

Easter Island is one of the most isolated inhabited islands in the world. It is in the southeastern Pacific, some 2,200 miles (3,500km) west of the Chilean coast of South America and 1,600 miles (2,600km) east of the island of Mangareva in the French Polynesian islands of the South Pacific. Linguistic evidence indicates that the first Polynesian settlers on Easter Island probably came from Mangareva, sailing across the vast expanse of the Pacific Ocean in outrigger canoes. They had arrived by about 1200 and began to develop a distinctive culture that diverged from the cultures of other Polynesian islands.

The greatest impact the settlers had on the island was deforestation, whether by cutting down trees for timber and clearing land for farming, or as a consequence of inadvertently introducing rats to the island, which prevented forests regenerating by eating the seeds and saplings of the trees. Some archaeologists think that the erection of the moai contributed to the deforestation because large quantities of wood were needed to transport the huge carved stones from quarries located on the side of the extinct volcano in the middle of the island to the so-called *apu*. These were stone platforms on which the moai were erected, most of which were near the coast. Other

ABOVE: Moai on the slopes of Rano Raraku, the extinct volcano on Easter Island where the stone used to make the statues was quarried.

research suggests that, rather than using wooden rollers to move the moai, the statues were "walked" to their positions by being kept upright and rocked from side to side to shuffle them forward. Whatever method was used to move the moai, considerable effort was clearly expended in erecting them. Around nine hundred originally stood around the island and many more have been found unfinished in the quarry or apparently abandoned by the sides of the roads from the quarries to the coast. The moai originally had red hats made from a different type of stone and eyes made from coral. All of the statues that were still standing when Europeans first arrived on the island were toppled in the 19th century; any that can be seen standing today were later reerected.

Collapse and Contact

In the collapse theory, the deforestation of Easter Island is said to have accelerated as the population rose, exposing the cleared ground to wind erosion and making it increasingly difficult to produce enough food as the soils degraded. Rather than address this problem, the elites of the island put even greater effort into erecting more and larger moai, thought to have represented the ancestors of the islanders and who were supposed to watch over their descendants. With resources running short, fighting is then said to have broken out between the clans who occupied different parts of the island and this, together with the shortage of food, led to a collapse in population from a peak estimated to have been 15,000 to perhaps 3,000 at the time of the European discovery of the island.

In recent years, archaeologists have challenged this collapse theory, some of them claiming that the scale of what happened on Easter Island has been exaggerated to highlight the impact of ignoring overexploitation of the environment. While acknowledging that deforestation and soil erosion would have had damaging consequences, they think the estimates of the peak population are far too high and that, rather than there being a collapse, there was a gradual decline.

THE BIRDMAN CULT

Tangata manu, or the birdman cult, was dedicated to the god Makemake and is thought to have developed on Easter Island after the erection of the moai had stopped. It involved an annual competition between the island's clans to collect the first sooty tern egg laid on the islet of Motu Nui. Each leader nominated a contestant to swim out to the islet. Once a contestant found an egg, they shouted out and, after swimming back to Easter Island, climbed to the top of a cliff to present the egg to their patron. The patron was then declared the winner and went on to perform various sacred duties over the course of the following year.

Little evidence of violence has been found anywhere on the island and it has also been suggested that the erection of the moai did not involve clans competing with each other. In reality, they are more likely to have cooperated in communal efforts to quarry, move, and then erect the statues, and this would have had beneficial effects on society by bringing it together for the common good.

It is now thought that more damage was done to the society of Easter Island after European contact, when infectious diseases were introduced to which the people on the island had no immunity. In the 1860s, as many as half of the entire population was abducted by Peruvian slavers to work as forced labor on plantations and in guano mines in Peru. By the time Chile annexed the island in 1888, fewer than two hundred people were still living there. Since that time, the population has recovered and now stands at almost eight thousand, split between indigenous people and Chilean incomers. The history of the island still has lessons to teach us about the impact of environmental degradation, but also, perhaps, about the dangers of jumping to conclusions when not in possession of all the facts. The people of Rapa Nui may have caused problems for themselves before they first encountered Europeans, but what came afterward appears to have been a whole lot worse.

BELOW: Hanga Roa, the capital of Easter Island today. The island's population has finally recovered after being decimated in the 19th century.

What Happened to the Lost Colony of Roanoke Island?

Where: North Carolina, USA

When: 1587

What: The first English attempt to colonize America

Comment: Fate unknown

ABOVE: The Virginia Dare Monument at Fort Raleigh, the modern name for the site of the Lost Colony on Roanoke Island, now a National Historic Site.

Roanoke Island is on the landward side of the Outer Banks, a long string of islands and spits separating the coast of North Carolina and the Atlantic Ocean. It is also the site of the first attempt to establish a permanent English settlement in North America. The failure of this mission was discovered when a long-delayed supply ship arrived at the settlement to find it completely deserted, and with only cryptic clues left behind as to what had happened there. The fate of the Lost Colony has never been established.

The Colony

The first attempt at establishing a settlement on Roanoke Island came in 1585 at the instigation of Sir Walter Raleigh, who had obtained a charter from English Queen Elizabeth I to that end, but did not actually take part in the venture himself. Motives were both commercial and to counter Spanish colonization of the continent of North America. The move was part of a long-running dispute between England and Spain that was partly concerned with exploiting the commercial opportunities opening up through the colonization of the New World and partly caused by the religious divide between Protestant England and Catholic Spain. A permanent settlement would also provide a base from which English privateers could attack Spanish treasure fleets as they returned to Spain from the New World.

ABOVE: A portrait of the English courtier and explorer Sir Walter Raleigh, painted in 1588— not long after the colony he sponsored on Roanoke Island was established.

The first settlement attempted to establish a garrison on the northern tip of the island, but hostile relations with the Native Americans, and no sign of a supply ship from England, led to the colony being abandoned in 1586. On that occasion, Sir Francis Drake stopped at the island on his way back to England from the Caribbean and offered passage to the colonists. The supply ship arrived some time later and, on finding the garrison deserted, left fifteen soldiers to man it while the ship returned to England. The following year, Raleigh sponsored a second attempt, led by John White—an artist who painted watercolors and made sketches while in America that are now held in the British Museum.

The ships carrying the new colonists arrived at Roanoke Island in the summer of 1587 to find that the garrison had disappeared without trace. The original intention appears to have been to pick up the soldiers of the garrison and continue on to Chesapeake Bay to the north, where a new settlement was to be founded. For unknown reasons, the plan changed. The ships remained at Roanoke Island for several months, after which 115 colonists were left there and the ships returned to England. John White also returned to England with the intention of organizing a supply ship to sail back out to the settlement as soon as possible. He left his daughter and son-in-law on the island, together with their newborn daughter Virginia Dare, now regarded as the first English person to be born in America.

Lost in America

By the time John White got back to England, in 1588, hostilities between England and Spain had escalated. In the summer of that year King Philip II of Spain famously sent the ill-fated Spanish Armada to invade England with the intention of dethroning Elizabeth I and restoring Catholicism in the country. The following year, the rather less known and equally unsuccessful English Armada set out to attack Spain. These conflicts prevented John White from being able to secure ships to return to Roanoke Island before 1590. When he finally did so, three years after he had left, he found that the settlement had been deserted.

JAMESTOWN

In 1607, English settlers established Jamestown, some 35 miles (55km) up the James River from Chesapeake Bay in what is now the state of Virginia. The site was not well chosen; the land was swampy and unsuitable for farming and the water supply was brackish. The settlement only survived the first winter with the help of the local Native American tribes and in the winter of 1609 around eighty percent of the colony's five hundred inhabitants died during the so-called "starving time." The colony survived but later abandoned the town, now a National Historic Site in which only the ruined brick tower of the church remains.

RIGHT: The ruined brick tower of the church in Jamestown, the only building still standing at the site.

Before returning to England in 1587, White had arranged for the remaining settlers to leave a sign if they had been forced to abandon the settlement—a Maltese cross carved into a tree. Upon his return, however, he found no such sign. The only clues to the whereabouts of the settlers, including those members of his family who had stayed on, were the word CROATOAN carved into the wooden palisade wall of the settlement and the letters C R O that were carved into a tree. The Croatoan were a nearby Native American tribe who lived on what the settlers knew as Croatoan Island, now called Hatteras Island. White took the carvings to mean that everybody had moved to the island to live with the Croatoan people.

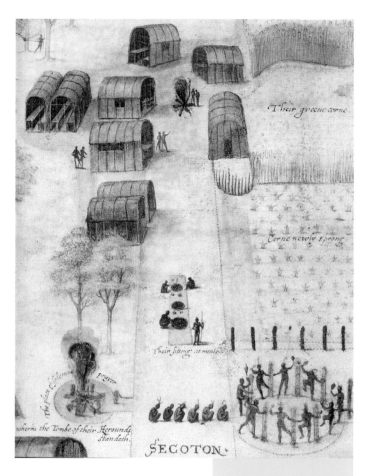

An approaching storm prevented White from staying in the area to search Croatoan Island and the ship he was sailing on left Roanoke Island to return to England. It was not until 12 years later that an attempt was made to find the settlers, but to no avail. That they had joined the Croatoan people remains the most likely explanation for what happened to them. In the four centuries since the Lost Colony went missing, various other attempts have been made to find them—including, in recent years, the genetic testing of the descendants of the Croatoans in an effort to establish whether the settlers integrated with the tribe. As yet, nothing has been found. Various artifacts claiming to be associated with the settlers have turned up over the years, but none have had anything to do with the Lost Colony. After such a long time, the chances of establishing what happened to the settlers are now remote and it is likely the Lost Colony will stay that way.

ABOVE: This watercolor, painted by John White in 1585, depicts Secoton, a Native American village on Roanoke Island when the English colony was first established.

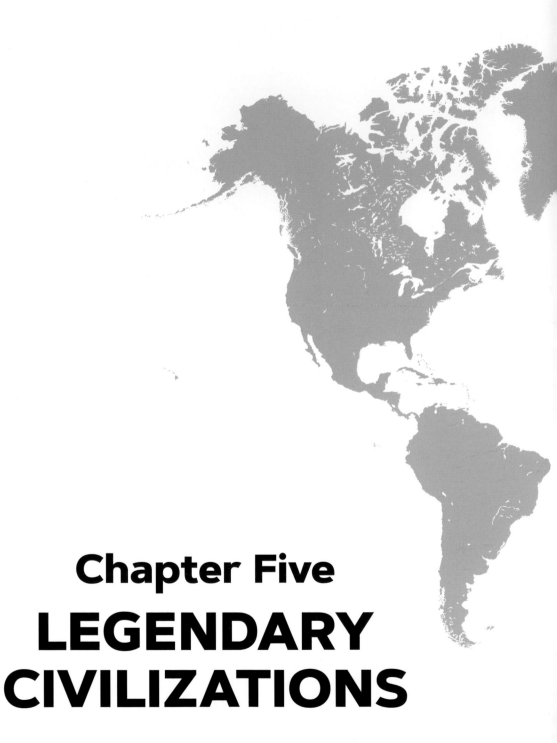

Chapter Five
LEGENDARY CIVILIZATIONS

Asgard

Hyperborea

Avalon

Atlantis

Shambhala

Lemuria

With previous chapters surveying lost civilizations that are known to have existed, we now take an opportunity to consider what might qualify as civilizations of the imagination. These are the places described in myths and legends, such as Atlantis and Hyperborea. Not only are these civilizations lost, but there is a good chance they never actually existed in the first place.

Did Atlantis Really Exist?

Where:	The Atlantic Ocean
When:	ca. 9400 BCE
What:	A lost continent
Comment:	Invented for allegorical purposes by the Greek philosopher Plato

ABOVE: A fresco depicting a harbor scene with boats from the Minoan town of Akrotiri, which was destroyed by the Thera eruption.

The story of the lost continent of Atlantis tells how an advanced civilization became submerged under the ocean. It is a familiar tale today, recounted by pseudo-historians who rarely allow facts to get in the way of a good story. It would be easy to dismiss such tales as works of fantasy had the story of Atlantis not first been told by the Greek philosopher Plato, now considered one of the three founding fathers of Western philosophy, along with Socrates and Aristotle. So, is there any truth to the story?

Plato's Atlantis

Plato wrote about Atlantis some time around 360 BCE in his later works, *Timaeus* and the unfinished *Critias*, the first two parts of an intended trilogy in which the final part was to be called *Hermacratus*, although Plato does not appear to have started writing it. The existing works were written in Plato's preferred form, the Socratic dialogue, in which he purports to be recording discussions held between his former teacher Socrates and other characters, in this case Timaeus, Critias, and Hermacratus. It is difficult to know for certain what Plato intended to achieve in these late works because the overall project was unfinished, but they appear to continue an examination of the notion of statehood and the creation of a just society that Plato had begun in the *Republic*. The final part of that work involved Socrates discussing several hypothetical cities governed in a variety of different ways as a means of examining what might constitute an ideal method of governance.

ABOVE: A Roman copy of a lost Greek bust of Plato by the sculptor Silanion. The original was commissioned by the Academy, the school founded by Plato in Athens.

In his dialogues, Plato wrote about a long-forgotten war between Athens and Atlantis, which occurred 9,000 years before the period in which he was writing. He described Atlantis as a much bigger and more powerful state than Athens, located on an island "beyond the pillars of Hercules," the two promontories on either side of the Strait of Gibraltar. These promontories are, to the north, the Rock of Gibraltar and, on the southern side of the strait, most likely either Jebel Musa in Morocco or Monte Hacho in Ceuta, the Spanish enclave on the North African coast. In other words, Plato was saying that Atlantis was out in the Atlantic Ocean. Unfortunately for those people who have since tried to find it, however, he didn't get any more specific.

LEFT: The Rock of Gibraltar, one of the pillars of Hercules mentioned by Plato, which marks the strait between the Mediterranean Sea and the Atlantic Ocean.

Atlantis attacked Athens from the sea and, despite being the more powerful state, was defeated. The Atlanteans, Plato wrote, had expected to win the war easily and it was this overconfidence that led to their downfall. Then, once the war was over, earthquakes and floods destroyed Atlantis, after which it sank into the ocean and disappeared. In describing this destruction, Plato was attempting to use Atlantis as an allegory for the Athens of his own time, which he thought had become bloated and corrupt. Through its own self-regard, he thought, the city was at risk of suffering the same fate as Atlantis if it did not change its ways. The inspiration for this story is not known, but Plato may have been looking back to the Peloponnesian War, fought between Athens and Sparta during his childhood some seventy years previously. Before the war, Athens had been the strongest of the Greek city-states, but in the end it was defeated by Sparta in a decisive naval battle.

The Modern Atlantis

During the Renaissance period that began in Italy during the 14th century, the rediscovery of the works of the classical philosophers brought Plato's writing back to light. It would not be until the late 19th century, however, that Atlantis began to take on a number of the characteristics ascribed to it today, including the idea that it harbored an advanced civilization that, before it sank into the Atlantic Ocean, was responsible for constructing such ancient wonders as the pyramids of Egypt and England's Stonehenge.

UTOPIA

In 1516, Sir Thomas More, the future Lord High Chancellor of England during the reign of King Henry VIII, published *Utopia*, a novel set on a fictional island of the same name in the New World. Following on from Plato, More set his imaginary island up as an ideal state and this allowed him to point out the faults in contemporary English society, in particular with the Catholic Church. The word "utopia" is now used in English to describe any idyllic place, though, so far at least, nobody has proposed that More's Utopia really existed or has gone in search of it off the coast of the Americas.

RIGHT: Sir Thomas More.

Such modern ideas can be traced back to the work of Ignatius L. Donnelly, an American lawyer and congressman of Irish descent. In 1882, Donnelly published *Atlantis: The Antediluvian World*, in which he claimed that Plato's lost island was in fact an entire continent on which civilization had first arisen and, among many other things, where the Garden of Eden was located. He went on to describe how a great flood had destroyed Atlantis and how folk memories of this cataclysm would resurface in such stories as the biblical account of Noah's Ark. Some of the few people who managed to escape Atlantis before it was overwhelmed by water settled, according to Donnelly, in Ireland, where they established a race of red-haired supermen.

Donnelly may have used Plato's account of Atlantis as his starting point, but he took the story in an entirely different direction—one that had little or nothing to do with the work of the classical philosopher. Nevertheless, his book would prove to be influential, impressing such well-known figures as Helena Blavatsky, who founded the Theosophical Society and whose work became one of the inspirations in the development of New Age spiritualism. The Austrian philosopher and mystic Rudolf Steiner, who developed the Waldorf system of

THE EMPIRE OF ATLANTIS.

education and biodynamic farming, was also influenced by Donnelly, as was the American spiritualist and psychic healer Edgar Cayce. In more recent times, an entire publishing genre has emerged, in which such authors as Graham Hancock and Andrew Collins have developed alternative theories explaining how numerous ancient archaeological sites are really evidence of a lost advanced civilization. Such theories are dismissed as psuedo-archaeology by mainstream academia because they are not based on the interpretation of actual archaeological discoveries. Nevertheless they have found a wide popular readership, perhaps reflecting the failure of academic archaeologists to explain their work in a straightforward and comprehensible way.

The renewed interest in Atlantis sparked by Donnelly and subsequent writers led to speculation on the location of Atlantis and numerous claims that it had been found. Donnelly himself thought that the Azores were the most likely candidate, a volcanic island group some 900 miles (1,500km) off the coast of Portugal. Geological surveys of the ocean floor around the islands have determined that the volcanic activity that created the islands occurred on an undersea plateau at a depth of more than 6,000ft (2,000m) and that this plateau has remained at roughly the same depth for the past twenty million years.

ABOVE: A map from *Atlantis: The Antediluvian World* by Ignatius L. Donnelly. According to the author, this shows the extent of the Atlantean Empire.

Other proposed locations of Atlantis have included the Canary Islands, the Bahamas, Cuba, mudbanks off the coast of Spain, and a host of other candidates, most of which are as easy to dismiss as the Azores and share the common thread of appearing to be more the products of wishful thinking than the facts on the ground. In one theory, archaeologists have attempted to engage with the speculation surrounding Atlantis by proposing that Plato was inspired by knowledge of the enormous volcanic eruption on the Aegean island of Thera, which is also considered a potential candidate for the destruction of the Minoan civilization on Crete.

The advantage of the Thera theory is that there is both geological and archaeological evidence for the eruption of the volcano and subsequent destruction of the Minoans, even if no indication exists that the event was known during the classical period. But Thera, or Santorini as it is now known, is in the wrong place, being east of Athens in the Aegean Sea rather than in the Atlantic Ocean, and the eruption occurred around 1,200 years before Plato's time rather than the 9,000 years he specified. Altogether, the Thera theory gives the impression of being little more than another attempt to bend the known facts to fit Plato's description, putting it in much the same category as all the other speculation. What we are left with, then, is the conclusion that Atlantis, as much as some people want to believe it really existed, is a lost civilization of the imagination, invented by Plato to make a particular point about the Athenian society of his own time and not based on anything in the real world.

BELOW: The view from the town of Fira on the Aegean island of Santorini. The headlands in the distance show the extent of the caldera left by the Thera eruption.

Is Lemuria a Sunken Continent Beneath the Indian Ocean?

Where: The Indian Ocean

When: First proposed in 1864 as a scientific theory

What: A lost continent

Comment: A geological impossibility

If the Atlantic Ocean can have a lost continent such as Atlantis hiding beneath its waves, can this also be the case for other oceans? It would seem so, because Lemuria is exactly that, a continent lost under the Indian Ocean. Where Atlantis was first described by Plato, the existence of Lemuria was initially proposed as a serious scientific theory in a paper published in 1864 by the British lawyer and zoologist Philip Lutley Sclater. Although his theory failed to stand up to scrutiny, by the time it had been discredited, the idea of Lemuria had taken on a life of its own.

ABOVE: Philip Lutley Sclater, the Victorian naturalist who first proposed the existence of Lemuria as a possible explanation for the distribution of lemurs.

Lemur Island

Philip Lutley Sclater was a Victorian gentleman naturalist, who, like his contemporary Charles Darwin, conducted his own research without ever holding a university position. He was a fellow of several prestigious societies, including the Royal Society and the Zoological Society of London, and published more than one thousand scientific papers. He had a particular interest in the geographical distribution of animals and, in a paper published in 1864 in the *Quarterly Journal of Science*, he discussed the lemurs of Madagascar. At the time, it was thought the lemur family also included the African galagos and the lorises of India. As there were many more species of lemurs than there were of galagos and lorises, Sclater proposed that the entire family had originated in Madagascar and had then spread out to Africa and Asia across a now sunken land bridge, or possibly an entire continent that had once connected all three.

Sclater proposed the name Lemuria for this sunken land and later modified his theory to exclude Africa, presumably after it became clear that lemurs and galagos are not that closely related. Given the scientific knowledge of the time, Sclater's theory was a reasonably sensible solution to the problem of lemur

BELOW: Sclater's lemur, named after Philip Lutley Sclater. The species is now critically endangered because much of its forest habitat on Madagascar has been cleared for farming.

distribution, but it turned out to be wrong in every respect. In 1912, the German geophysicist Alfred Wegener proposed the theory of continental drift, based on the premise that continental landmasses cannot sink because they are largely made up of a type of rock that is not as dense as the rock of the mantle below. Wegener thought the continents had once been part of a single supercontinent, which had split as the landmasses drifted apart on the mantel. His ideas were later modified so that, rather than continents drifting, the plates making up the whole of the Earth's crust moved, a theory that became known as "plate tectonics."

We now know that Africa, Madagascar, and India really were part of a supercontinent that split as the different plates on which they rested drifted apart. Madagascar and India split from Africa around 135 million years ago and then, 88 million years ago, Madagascar and India also split, as the Indian plate drifted northward until it crashed into the Eurasian plate. Madagascar, then, has been an island for a very long time, and its distinctive animals and plants have evolved in isolation. Lemurs actually arrived on the island around twenty million years after the split with India. The animals originally came from Africa, with an ancestral species having crossed the 260 miles (420km) of the Mozambique Channel after being swept out to sea on a raft of vegetation. Once in Madagascar, and with little competition from other mammals, the lemurs evolved into numerous different species, including the now critically endangered Sclater's lemur.

From Lemurs to Lemurians

A few years after Sclater came up with the concept of Lemuria, the German biologist Ernst Haeckel borrowed the idea to propose that the sunken continent was the location of the so-called "missing link" in human evolution, a transitional species between apes and humans, the fossils of which, according to Haeckel, had not been found because the rocks bearing them were lost beneath the Indian Ocean. He went on to expand this theory by suggesting that humans first

MAURITIA

Geologists think that, when Madagascar and India split apart 88 million years ago, a fragment of the original supercontinent remained in the Indian Ocean until it was covered eight million years ago by lava from a series of massive underwater volcanic eruptions that formed the island of Mauritius. On the beautiful beaches of Mauritius, they have found crystals of the mineral zircon that are hundreds of millions of years older than the island itself and that can only have come from the remnants of what they have named as the microcontinent of Mauritia. It isn't Lemuria and it disappeared beneath lava not seawater, but, nevertheless, it's a piece of lost continent in the Indian Ocean.

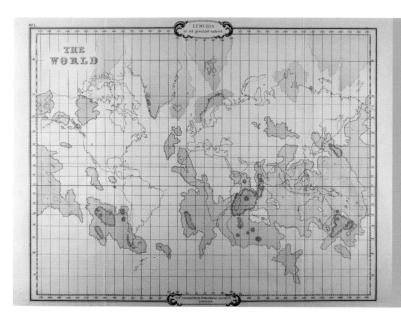

LEFT: This map from *The Lost Lemuria* (1904) by the theosophist William Scott-Elliot details the full extent of Lemuria, shown in pink as spanning the globe.

evolved in Lemuria before spreading out to Africa and Asia, writing in 1876, "The probable primeval home or 'paradise' is here assumed to be Lemuria, a tropical continent at present lying below the level of the Indian Ocean," and going on to describe Lemuria as being the "cradle of the human race."

The idea of a lost continent playing a central role in human evolution led to the existence of Lemuria being embraced by many of the same people who had popularized the Atlantis story. Principle among these was Helena Blavatsky, who published *The Secret Doctrine* in 1888; in the work, she claimed to be passing on mystical knowledge she had received while traveling in Tibet, from people she described as the "mahatmas." Today, the book reads as a mix of Eastern mysticism and Western occultism with some ideas taken from evolutionary biology, but also some from pure fantasy. According to Blavatsky, humanity was composed of seven "root races," the third of which were the Lemurians, who she described as being 7-ft-tall (2.1m) egg-laying hermaphrodites and who were not very bright, but were spiritually pure. It may have been nonsense, but it was taken up enthusiastically by her followers and elaborated upon so that a theory that had started out as an attempt to explain the distribution of lemurs was transformed into an answer for what Douglas Adams called "the ultimate question of life, the Universe, and everything." Unfortunately for Blavatsky and her followers, plate tectonics have shown that Lemuria is not the answer to anything at all, not even the distribution of lemurs.

Were Avalon and King Arthur Real?

Where: Great Britain, Europe

When: Sometime around 500 CE

What: The Isle of Apples

Comment: Founded in legend

ABOVE: Detail from a tapestry made in ca. 1385, showing King Arthur as one of the Nine Worthies, figures from history who set the standard for chivalrous behavior.

In the aftermath of the sixth century Battle of Camlann, at which King Arthur was mortally wounded fighting against the invading Saxons, the enchantress Morgen took the monarch to Avalon, the Isle of Apples. It is believed that, one day when his country needs him most, Arthur will return. At least, that is the story according to medieval chronicler Geoffrey of Monmouth. Yet no records or artifacts have survived that might confirm Arthur's existence, nor does anything point toward the location of his final resting place. So, what can we say about Avalon today?

The Legend Begins

The Arthurian legends are set in the period after the Romans withdrew from Britain, conventionally said to have occurred in 410 CE, though, in reality, the withdrawal probably occurred over a much longer time frame. As the Roman Empire weakened, Britain struggled to defend itself against incursions of Germanic tribes from northern Europe, generally referred to as the Saxons, and it is against this background that the Arthurian legends arise.

King Arthur is portrayed as the leader of the British forces fighting against the Saxons in the late fifth and early sixth centuries. None of the few surviving contemporary historical sources mention a king by that name, though Gildas, a monk writing around 530, does describe battles between British and Saxon armies. Arthur is named, however, as a military leader rather than a king in the *Historia Brittonum* (*The History of the Britons*), a compilation of historical writings from around 828, sometimes attributed to the Welsh monk Ninnius. Such sources provided a basis for Geoffrey of Monmouth's *Historia Regum Britanniae* (*The History of the Kings of Britain*), written around 1138, and in which he appears to have filled in the gaps using his own imagination so as to present a narrative of King Arthur's life.

ABOVE: A page from a late-12th-century, French, illuminated manuscript of Geoffrey of Monmouth's *Historia Regum Britanniae*.

Many of the elements we now associate with Arthur are present in Geoffrey of Monmouth's book, including Merlin the magician, Guinevere, Excalibur, and Avalon. In later years, such writers as Chrétien de Troyes and Sir Thomas Malory embroidered their Arthurian romances with tales not found in Geoffrey's work, including the Knights of the Round Table, Camelot, the love affair between Lancelot and Guinevere, and the quest for the Holy Grail. Attempting to establish what, if anything, was based on historical truth and what was pure invention is an impossible task today.

Glastonbury

Geoffrey of Monmouth does not tell us where Avalon can be found beyond describing it as being reached by boat. Around fifty years after Geoffrey wrote

CAMELOT

Geoffrey of Monmouth thought King Arthur held his court at Caerleon, now a small town in South Wales. Chrétien de Troyes, writing in the late 1170s, provided us with the name of Camelot and also mentioned Caerleon, though later English writers preferred locations in England such as Winchester, where Anglo-Saxon kings sometimes held their courts, or Cadbury Castle, an Iron Age hill fort in Somerset. Tintagel Castle in Cornwall also has a claim, though the legends say this is where Arthur was born not where he held his court. In fact, the ruins in this beautiful spot by the sea are actually those of a medieval castle.

LEFT: The ruins of the medieval Tintagel Castle. Whatever Arthurian connections it may have, the castle sits in a beautiful spot on the coast of north Cornwall.

his account, the rather more reliable Gerald of Wales recorded the discovery of Arthur's grave by monks at Glastonbury Abbey, the ruins of which can be seen today in the English county of Somerset. Gerald's description indicates that he was present when a coffin made from a hollowed-out oak tree was found during a search of the abbey grounds. It was buried 15ft (5m) below ground, in what Gerald says was an effort to hide it from the Saxons. When the coffin was raised, a stone slab was found underneath it on which a lead cross had been attached bearing the inscription, "Here in the island of Avalon lies the renowned King Arthur with Guinevere, his second wife."

Gerald tells us that the old Welsh name for Glastonbury was Ynys Afallach, Island of Apples, and that it was surrounded by low-lying marshland that was frequently inundated by the sea. The marshland, known as the Somerset Levels, has been drained so that Glastonbury is now firmly on dry land, the only indication of its island past coming on misty mornings when Glastonbury

Tor, a hill near the site, can give the impression of rising up through the mist, as if it is floating.

The coffin was later reburied within the abbey and subsequently moved when the interior of the building was changed in 1368 so that the choir stalls could be extended. In 1539, the abbey was dissolved as part of the Dissolution of the Monasteries ordered by King Henry VIII and the location of the reburial was lost. Today, historians think that the monks of the abbey most likely concocted the entire story to raise money to repair the abbey after it had been extensively damaged by fire.

Numerous stories have sprung up about Glastonbury over the years, prominent among them being that Joseph of Arimathea, who presided over the burial of Christ after the Crucifixion, came to Glastonbury, bringing the Holy Grail with him. King Arthur may or may not have existed and Glastonbury may or may not have been Avalon. Nevertheless this should not detract from the enjoyment to be had from reading the stories.

BELOW: Glastonbury Tor has been associated with numerous legends and, according to some, was where King Arthur was buried after being mortally wounded in battle.

Was Shambhala a Real Place?

Where:	Tibet, Asia
When:	For all time
What:	A mythical kingdom
Comment:	Exists outside of this Earthly realm

ABOVE: An illustration of Shambhala, in the shape of a lotus blossom surrounded by snow-peaked mountains and with Kalapa, its capital city, at the center.

In the sacred texts of Tibetan Buddhism, Shambhala is a mythical kingdom, a paradise or pure land in which people live in peace and harmony. It is described in the Kalachakra Tantra, one of the three Wheels of Time teachings, as existing in the shape of the eight petals of a lotus flower surrounded by snowcapped mountains and with a crystal mountain that stands next to a sacred lake at its middle, marking the entrance to the capital city of Kalapa. Similar places appear in Hindu texts and in the beliefs of Bon, the ancient religion of Tibet, thought to have been practiced prior to the arrival of Buddhism.

The Spiritual Paradise

The Dalai Lama, the spiritual leader of Tibetan Buddhism, has said that Shambhala is not a physical place, but can be reached at the end of a spiritual journey. In the West, some people interested in Eastern religions have argued that the mythical Shambhala was originally a real place somewhere in the remote Himalayas; the more romantic among them have described it as a lost valley of peace and tranquility. One of these people was the Portuguese Jesuit missionary António de Andrade, who heard stories of a mysterious kingdom beyond the Himalayas in the 1620s, while at the court of the Mughal emperor Jahangir in the Indian city of Agra. The stories included descriptions of religious practices that made Andrade think that the people living there were a lost Christian community, so he set out to find them, in the process becoming the first known European traveler to journey into Tibet.

In 2004, the historian and television presenter Michael Wood followed in the footsteps of António de Andrade, traveling into western Tibet. His journey was not easy—at that time, the Mana Pass, the main route from India into western Tibet, was closed. Nevertheless, taking a long detour through Nepal and the odd ride in a helicopter, Wood made it to Tsaparang, the ruins of the ancient capital city of the Kingdom of Guge, now in the Ngari province in the far west of Tibet. It is not far from Mount Kailash, a 21,800ft (6,600m) mountain that is sacred in Bon, Buddhism, and Hinduism. Lake Manasarovar, also sacred, lies nearby, together with the sources of four great rivers: the Indus, the Brahmaputra, the Sutlej, and the Karnali, a tributary of the Ganges.

BELOW: The sacred mountain, Mount Kailash, is an object of pilgrimage for Buddhists and Hindus. They show their devotion by walking around it but never setting foot on it.

The sacred geography of the region led Wood to speculate that Tsaparang, Mount Kailash, and Lake Manasarovar could have been the inspiration for Tagzig Olmo Lung Ring, the name in the Bon tradition for what Tibetan Buddhists call Shambhala. Wood did not suggest that it was the earthly manifestation of such divine places and, in truth, the region does not exactly match what most of us would consider to be paradise. Lake Manasarovar is at an elevation of 15,000ft (4,500m) and the climate is cold and dry, so there is not a great deal of vegetation in the region. It looks barren and inhospitable, hardly the land of plenty where the trees are laden with fruit and the fields full of grain. Living here must always have been hard and perhaps that is why the path to spiritual enlightenment leads toward a paradise where the everyday struggles of life are over and where people live in peace and harmony.

THE GARDEN OF EDEN

In the Hebrew Bible, Adam and Eve are expelled from paradise, the Garden of Eden, after eating the forbidden fruit. The book of Genesis describes the sources of four rivers within the Garden of Eden, and though no mountains or lakes are mentioned, the parallels with Shambhala are obvious enough. In Christianity, paradise can be regained through the saving grace of God, while in Buddhism, it is reached by the spiritual journey to enlightenment. Whatever your faith, it would appear unlikely that paradise will be found on a trekking holiday to the Himalayas to look for a lost valley.

LEFT: *The Garden of Eden*, painted in 1503 by the German artist Lucas Cranach the Elder.

Shangri-La

In 1933, the British author James Hilton published the novel *Lost Horizons*, a story of the survivors of a plane crash in the western Himalayas who are rescued by local people and taken to a Buddhist monastery named Shangri-La. The monastery is in a beautiful valley under a snowcapped mountain, isolated from the rest of the world and where people live in harmony with each other. The depiction of lives being lived in peace and tranquility in this lost valley appears to have struck a chord with people who were then enduring the height of the Great Depression. It was also published fifteen years after the end of the First World War—a time when fascism was on the rise in Europe and Adolf Hitler had just seized power in Germany.

Today, *Lost Horizons* is remembered for introducing the word Shangri-la into the English language, which means a beautiful place of the imagination. The similarity of the name with Shambhala is apparent enough, though Hilton did not ever explicitly say that he took his inspiration from Tibetan Buddhist teachings. He did cite the books of two French missionaries, Évariste Régis Huc and Joseph Gabet, who had traveled through western Tibet in the 19th century and, as a English translation of António de Andrade's work was published in 1926, we can guess that he had read this as well. Whatever the case, the thought of Shangri-la or Shambhala exisiting as an actual place on Earth is an attractive one. Whether we are familiar with Tibetan Buddhist teachings or not, who wouldn't want to live in a place that is free of the troubles of the outside world and where we can provide for ourselves without having to work too hard? We all know that such a place doesn't really exist in this Earthly realm, but it doesn't hurt to dream.

ABOVE: A poster for the 1937 film *Lost Horizon*, directed by Frank Capra. As well as Ronald Colman, the notable cast includes Jane Wyatt and Sam Jaffe.

Did Hyperborea Exist and Where Was It?

Where: North of Greece, Europe

When: Classical antiquity

What: A terra incognita

Comment: A place in the imagination of the Greeks

ABOVE: An illustration of the Greek myth of Orithyia being abducted by Boreas, god of the north wind. Hyperborea could be found beyond Boreas's homeland of Thrace.

To the ancient Greeks, Hyperborea was a place "beyond the north wind," and was inhabited by giants. Over the course of classical antiquity, numerous Greek and Roman writers described where they thought Hyperborea might have been located, but beyond a general agreement on it being somewhere to the north, most accounts of its whereabouts differ wildly. So, were the Greeks referring to somewhere specific or was Hyperborea just an attempt to describe the kind of world that might lie beyond the one they knew?

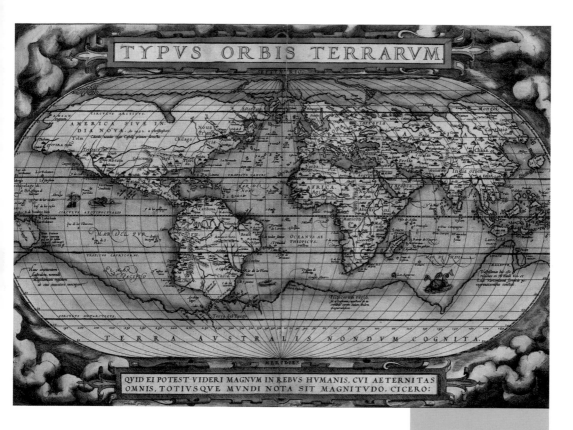

TYPVS ORBIS TERRARVM

QVID EI POTEST VIDERI MAGNVM IN REBVS HVMANIS, CVI AETERNITAS OMNIS, TOTIVSQVE MVNDI NOTA SIT MAGNITVDO. CICERO:

Terra Incognita

In Greek mythology, the Anemoi were the gods of the wind, each named for the direction from which the wind came. Boreas, god of the north wind and the bringer of winter, was said to live in the mountains of Thrace, the region to the north of Greece now made up of parts of Bulgaria and the European part of Turkey. In *The Histories*, the ancient Greek historian Herodotus reported that, in a now lost work, it had been Homer who had thought the Boreans came from Thrace. Herodotus went on to discuss the Hyperboreans, writing that, since the Boreans came from Thrace, the Hyperboreans must come from beyond Thrace. This led him to conclude that the Hyperboreans came from Dacia, on the northern side of the Danube River, in what is now Romania.

Herodotus was the first of the classical writers to provide a location for Hyperborea, but he was by no means the last. Over the centuries, the Greeks and Romans came up with numerous other possible places where the Hyperboreans lived, agreeing only that it was north of Greece and that it was beyond what they called the Riphean Mountains. Needless to say, the location of the Riphean Mountains was not specified either, making it difficult to locate

ABOVE: A map of the world from 1570. The work of the Dutch cartographer Abraham Ortelius, the map shows the unknown northern regions as a terra incognita similar to Hyperborea.

Hyperborea. They could, for example, refer to the Rhodope Mountains in southern Bulgaria or the Balkan Mountains across the middle of that country, or perhaps the Carpathian Mountains farther north, in Romania.

Pliny the Elder, the Roman author writing in the first century CE, some five hundred years after Herodotus, identified the Riphean Mountains with the Urals, the mountain range running south to north through Russia, pushing the location of Hyperborea way up north, beyond the Arctic Circle. This, perhaps, offers a clue as to what was going on. As the extent of the known world increased during the classical period, the terra incognita—the blank spaces on the map—were pushed farther and farther away from Greece and Rome. This meant that the mythological Hyperborea had to move with it; it could no longer be located in Dacia because the Greeks and Romans knew that the Dacians lived there. Strabo, writing in *Geographica* a few decades before Pliny, said: "It is because of men's ignorance of these regions that any heed has

THULE

According to the ancient Greeks, Hyperborea could be found beyond the north wind, but it was not the farthest northern place. This was called Thule, first recorded in a lost work from around 325 BCE by Pytheas of Massalia, which is only known to us today through references by other classical authors. Pytheas explored the northwest of

Europe, sailing around the British Isles and apparently claiming that Thule could be found by sailing for six days farther north. In his *Geographica*, Strabo quoted extensively from Pytheas, but wasn't any more impressed by the idea of Thule than he had been by Hyperborea, writing that he thought Pytheas had made it up.

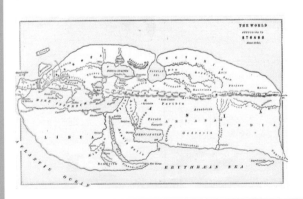

LEFT: An interpretation of the world as described by Strabo, who wrote about the known facts and had little time for fantasies invented to fill in the gaps.

been given to those who created the mythical Riphean Mountains and Hyperboreans," and went on to say that such writing should be disregarded.

Twisted Mythology

Rather than dismissing such mythology altogether, Strabo could have suggested that writers distinguish between geographic fact and mythological speculation, because much of what was written about Hyperborea before his day usually failed to make such a distinction. Most of the classical writers who described Hyperborea attempted to fill in the terra incognita with fabulous stories, safe in the knowledge that nobody else could contradict them. There are parallels to the ways in which later and contemporary pseudo-historians seize on subjects that are not fully understood to promote ideas that would not otherwise stand up to scrutiny. It may come as no surprise, therefore, to find that occultists and purveyors of esoteric mysticism have also made claims about the Hyperboreans, some of them quite dark.

ABOVE: The Rhodope Mountains of Bulgaria, lying to the north of Greece. They represent one of several possible locations of the mythical Riphean Mountains.

As the location of Hyperborea crept farther north, some of the later classical writers described the Hyperboreans as being tall and fair-haired. This was sufficient for such Nazi occultists as Heinrich Himmler—architect of the Holocaust—to pick up on and to manipulate into becoming one line of evidence to support the supposed superiority of the so-called Nordic race. The Nordic race, of whom the Germans deemed themselves the finest example, became fused with the Aryan race, which is not an obvious partnership because the Aryans originally came from central Asia and Iran. Nevertheless, this led the Nazi occultists to believe that Germans were Nordic-Aryans who were descended from the Hyperboreans. Although based on mythology, this was one of several views that contributed to the Nazis carrying out some of the worst crimes committed in history.

Where Is Asgard, Home of the Gods?

Where:	Scandinavia
When:	Before Christianity arrived in Scandinavia
What:	The realm of the gods
Comment:	Founded in Norse mythology

ABOVE: The one-eyed Norse god Odin riding Sleipnir, his eight-legged horse, as depicted in an 18th-century Icelandic manuscript.

I n Norse mythology, Asgard was the realm of the gods. It was described as being surrounded by walls and was where Valhalla, the great hall of the god Odin, could be found. What we know about Asgard today, and the Old Norse religion in general, primarily comes from a handful of sources mostly written after Scandinavia had converted to Christianity, together with what can be gathered from such archaeological remains as Viking burials. But, as the Norse civilization was mostly an oral one from which only a few runic inscriptions remain, a great amount of detail must also have been lost.

Snorri's Story

The two principle written sources from which much of our knowledge of the Norse religion comes are both Icelandic, and are known as the *Poetic Edda* and the *Prose Edda*. The *Poetic Edda* is a collection of what are thought originally to have been orally transmitted poems that were written down by anonymous scribes in the 13th century and collected together. The only extant primary source for these poems is the so-called Codex Regius, a manuscript that contains around half of the poems. The sources of the remaining poems were presumably similar manuscripts that have since been lost.

The *Prose Edda* was written by Snorri Sturluson, an Icelandic poet, historian, and politician working in the early 13th century. He is thought to have written this work around 1220, with the intention of providing other Icelandic poets with details of traditional Norse poetry. He recorded different poetic forms, the style of language used in traditional poetry, and provided details of Norse mythology and its pantheon of gods, presumably as a reference for those poets wanting to ensure their own attempts at traditional Norse poetry were correct. Snorri's *Edda* was, then, a writer's handbook, and while it is not clear how much use it was to the poets of Snorri's time, it has proved invaluable today as a source of information about Norse religion in the pre-Christian period.

BELOW: This title page from a 17th-century manuscript of the *Prose Edda*, shows Odin (top), together with other figures from Norse mythology.

The Norse religion was polytheistic and its gods and goddesses were divided into two groups, the Aesirs, including Thor and Odin, and the Vanirs, such as Njörðr, Freyr, and Freyja. Altogether, more than thirty gods and goddesses are named in the sources, which also describe a war between the Aesirs and the Vanirs started by Odin, who led an army to attack Vanaheimr, the home of the Vanirs. Over the course of a long and bitter conflict in which both sides inflicted terrible casualties on each other, it gradually became clear that neither was powerful enough to win. A truce was declared and the two sides exchanged hostages to ensure that the terms of the truce were maintained.

Asgard, the home of the Aesirs, and Vanaheimr are two of the nine worlds of Norse cosmology, which are connected together by Yggdrasil, the great tree of life. Unfortunately, the sources don't describe all of these nine worlds, but we do know that our own realm is called Midgard and that it is connected to Asgard by a bridge in the form of a rainbow. When a warrior was killed in battle, Odin took them to Asgard via this bridge and they then resided in Valhalla, where they occupied their time drinking beer and fighting with each other.

The Viking Age

The period between the ninth century and the Norman invasion of Britain in 1066 is sometimes called the Viking Age of European history—a time when large-scale Norse migrations began and Viking settlements formed across many different parts of the European continent. Today, we usually think of the Vikings as raiders of monasteries and abbeys on the east coast of the British Isles and, while this is certainly part of the story, they were also explorers, traders, and peaceful settlers who traveled as far west as Greenland and the coast of North America. They also journeyed through Russia and established trading links around the Mediterranean and with the Byzantine Empire in what is modern-day Turkey.

NORMAN SICILY

The Normans, descendants of Viking settlers and French people from Normandy, invaded Sicily in the late 11th century, establishing a kingdom that lasted a little over a hundred years. Some of the castles and churches on the island today date from that period and the architecture of these buildings shows how the Normans were influenced by the previous Byzantine and Arabic periods. A hybrid Norman-Arab-Byzantine culture developed, characterized by churches with Gothic windows and Islamic domes, which lasted until 1198, when Sicily was invaded by the Holy Roman Empire.

ABOVE: Pepoli Castle in Erice demonstrates the hybrid style of Sicilian architecture from the Norman period.

One consequence of the increasing contact between the Vikings and the rest of Europe was the exposure of the Norse to Christianity, in part through the work of Christian missionaries, but also by the contacts made through trade and the settlements established in Britain and France. In around 960, King Harald Bluetooth of Denmark and Norway erected a stone that stills stands in the town of Jelling, Denmark, with a runic inscription that tells how he had converted his realm to Christianity. The actual story appears to have been rather more complicated—Christianity appears to have been adopted gradually so that the old pagan beliefs persisted alongside Christian practices. Over the course of several centuries, the Old Norse religion and the worship of Odin, Thor, and all the other gods of Asgard faded away so that, by the time Snorri Sturluson wrote his handbook, people needed to be reminded of exactly who was who. The *Prose Edda* has also proved a godsend for popular culture today, influencing everything from comic strips to Hollywood movies, even if there is no actual evidence that any real Viking ever wore a helmet with horns on.

ABOVE: The Jelling stones in the Danish town of Jelling. Harald Bluetooth erected the larger of the two and his father, King Gorm the Old, erected the other.

Further Reading

Books

Anthony, David W. *The Horse, the Wheel, and Language: How Bronze-Age Riders from the Eurasian Steppes Shaped the Modern World.* Princeton: Princeton University Press, 2007.

Cline, Eric H. *1177 BC: The Year Civilization Collapsed.* Princeton: Princeton University Press, 2014.

Cunliffe, Barry. *By Steppe, Desert, and Ocean: The Birth of Eurasia.* Oxford: Oxford University Press, 2015.

Cunliffe, Barry. *Europe Between the Oceans: 9000 BC – AD 1000.* Oxford; New Haven: Yale University Press, 2008.

Darwin, John. *After Tamerlane: The Rise and Fall of Global Empires, 1400–2000.* London: Bloomsbury, 2008.

Diamond, Jared. *Collapse: How Societies Choose to Fail or Succeed.* London: The Viking Press, 2005.

Fagon, Brian. *The Long Summer: How Climate Changed Civilization.* New York: Basic Books, 2003.

Feng, Li. *Early China: A Social and Cultural History.* Cambridge: Cambridge University Press, 2013.

Forster, Benjamin R. *The Age of Agade: Inventing Empire in Ancient Mesopotamia.* Oxon: Routledge, 2016.

Frankopan, Peter. *The Silk Roads: A New History of the World.* London: Bloomsbury, 2015.

Hunt, Terry, and Carl Lipo. *The Statues that Walked: Unraveling the Mystery of Easter Island.* New York: Free Press, 2011.

Miles, Richard. *Ancient Worlds: The Search for the Origins of Western Civilization.* London: Allen Lane, 2010.

Parker, Philip (Ed.). *The Great Trade Routes: A History of Cargoes and Commerce Over Land and Sea.* Annapolis: US Naval Institute Press, 2012.

Robinson, Andrew. *The Indus: Lost Civilizations.* London: Reaktion Books, 2015.

Sagona, Anthony, and Paul Zimansky. *Ancient Turkey.* Oxon: Routledge, 2009.

Scott, James C. *Against the Grain: A Deep History of the Earliest States.* New Haven: Yale University Press, 2017.

Scott, Michael. *Ancient Worlds: An Epic History of East and West.* London: Hutchinson, 2017.

Shipley, Lucy. *The Etruscans: Lost Civilizations.* London: Reaktion Books, 2017.

Wood, Michael. *In Search of Myths and Heroes.* London: BBC Books, 2005.

Yoffee, Norman, and George L. Cowgill. *The Collapse of Ancient States and Civilizations.* Tucson: The University of Arizona Press, 1988.

Websites

The Ancient History Encyclopedia:
ancient.eu

Antiquity Journal:
antiquity.ac.uk

Archaeological sites on Malta:
visitmalta.com/en/archaeological-sites

BBC *In Our Time* radio series:
bbc.co.uk/programmes/b006qykl

The British Museum:
britishmuseum.org

The Cahokia Mounds State Historic Site:
cahokiamounds.org

Current World Archaeology magazine:
world-archaeology.com

Göbekli Tepe:
gobeklitepe.info

Historic Jamestowne:
historicjamestowne.org

The Hopi people of Arizona:
hopi-nsn.gov

The Kınık Höyük Archaeological Project:
kinikhoyuk.org

National Geographic magazine:
nationalgeographic.com

New Scientist magazine:
newscientist.com

The Smithsonian Museum:
smithsonianmag.com

Tintagel Castle:
english-heritage.org.uk/visit/places/tintagel-castle/

UNESCO World Heritage Sites:
whc.unesco.org/en/list/

Index

Acknowledgments

(t = top, m = middle, b = bottom, l = left, r = right)

Alamy Stock Photo: 11 World History Archive; 13 North Wind Picture Archives; 16 Phil Degginger; 20 & 143 Granger Historical Picture Archive; 31 & 52 PRIMSA ARCHIVO; 38 & 182 Science History Images; 42 & 98 INTERFOTO; 44 age fotostock; 45 Artokoloro Quint Lox Limited; 60 & 64 Danita Delimont; 66 & 126 robertharding; 80 funkyfood London – Paul Williams; 83 Historic Collection; 92 dpa picture archive; 100 www.BibleLandPictures.com; 101 Peter Horree; 109 The History Collection; 112 Godong; 113 The Picture Art Collection; 116 Karen Su/China Span; 118 Oscar Espinosa; 145 UK Alan King; 147 National Geographic Image Collection; 148 CarverMostardi; 160 History and Art Collection; 161t Erin Babnik; 169 Chronicle; 177 PictureLux/The Hollywood Archive; 180 Old Paper Studios.

Bridgeman Images: 174 *The Paradise of Shambhala*, Tibetan Banner (painted silk), Tibetan School/Musee Guimet, Paris, France.

The British Library, London: 171.

Dreamstime: 136 Ken Backer; 172 Aagje De Jong.

Getty Images: 10 Werner Forman/Universal Images Group; 18 & 39 DEA/G. Nimatallah; 35 De Agostini Picture Library; 54 Edoardo Frola; 63 Vivian Moos/Corbis; 74 Sovfoto/UIG via Getty Images; 134 Kryssia Campos; 140 Bettmann.

Library of Congress, Washington, D.C.: 89, 149, 164 & 179.

The Metropolitan Museum of Art, New York: 65, 70, 76, 78, 90, 95 & 111.

Shutterstock: 15 Robert Hoetink; 17 Karakol; 19 Warpaint; 22 ascen; 24 Brian C. Weed; 26 M Selcuk Oner; 27 Yasemin Olgunoz Berber; 28 Nila Newsom; 30 Serj Malomuzh; 32 CoolR; 33 Geza Farkas; 34 alanf; 36 Kakoli Dey; 37 CRS PHOTO; 40 suronin; 43 Jason Benz Bennee; 46 Jay75; 47 milan noga; 50 Luzerendering; 51 Szymon Kaczmarczyk; 53 blackboard1965; 56, 81 & 120 Danita Delmont; 57 Bill Perry; 59 Teddy Hung; 61 Fer Gregory; 62 Nathan Kelly; 72 VIIIPhotography; 73 Alexander Demyanov; 75 STJUHA; 77 Angelo Giampiccolo; 79 David Pineda Svenske; 84 Gernant Images; 86 Kanuman; 87 Yakov Oskanov; 91 Christian Vinces; 93 Inspired by Maps; 102 Martina Badini; 103 zaferkizilkaya; 104 Izabela Miszczak; 105 TheRunoman; 106 Gilmanshin; 108 Daniel Andis; 114 knovakov; 115 C. Na Songkhla; 119 Dmitry Chulov; 121 MosayMay; 122 Luciano Mortula – LGM; 124 Mukul Banerjee; 125 clicksabhi; 130 Brandon Bourdages; 131 Simon Dannhauer; 133 John_Walker; 137 Traveller70; 138 LOUIS-MICHEL DESERT; 139 Gimas; 142 Russ Heinl; 144 Agatha Kadar; 146 PhilipR; 150 Christian Wilkinson; 151 Olga Danylenko; 152 RPBaiao; 154 William Silver; 161b Dubassy; 162 anyaivanova; 165 Roman Sigaev; 173 Dave Porter; 175 Lihana; 181 Monumental Art; 184 Irina Sen; 185 lauradibi.

Wellcome Collection, London: 178 (CC BY 4.0).

Wikimedia Commons: 25 Klaus-Peter Simon (CC BY SA-3.0); 69 Liveon001 © Travis Witt (CC BY SA-3.0); 132 Sébastian Homberger (CC BY 2.5); 141 Number 57 at English Wikipedia (CC0 1.0); 155 National Portrait Gallery; 156 Tony Fischer (CC BY 2.0); 163 The Frick Collection (Accession Number: 1912.1.77); 167 Charlie Marshall (CC BY 2.0).